KENMORE MICROWAVE COOKING

Sears

A Benjamin Company Book

Associate Publishers: Robert C. Dougherty, Beth Kukkonen
Editor: Ellyn Polshek
Production Assistants: Pat Drew, Susan Jablonski
Chief Home Economist: Betty Sullivan
Consulting Home Economists: Thelma Pressman, Susan K. Ribordy,
    Dora Jonassen, Maggie Fagan, Irene Falk, Sharon Kahn,
    Gloria Kelly, Joan McClain, Mary Lou Merritt, Debbie Moore,
    Marianne Olix, Gerry Paxson, Marcia Schwall
Project Manager: M. K. Duncan
Art & Design: Thomas C. Brecklin
Typography: A-Line, Milwaukee
Photography: Walter Storck

USER INSTRUCTIONS

PRECAUTIONS TO AVOID POSSIBLE EXPOSURE TO EXCESSIVE MICROWAVE ENERGY

(a) DO NOT ATTEMPT to operate this oven with the door open since open-door operation can result in harmful exposure to microwave energy. It is important not to defeat or tamper with the safety interlocks.

(b) DO NOT PLACE any object between the oven front face and the door or allow soil or cleaner residue to accumulate on sealing surfaces.

(c) DO NOT OPERATE the oven if it is damaged. It is particularly important that the oven door closes properly and that there is no damage to the:
> (1) DOOR (bent)
> (2) HINGES AND LATCHES (broken or loosened)
> (3) DOOR SEALS AND SEALING SURFACES

(d) THE OVEN SHOULD NOT BE ADJUSTED OR REPAIRED BY ANYONE EXCEPT PROPERLY QUALIFIED SERVICE PERSONNEL.

Library of Congress Catalog Card Number: 78-71995
ISBN: 0-87502-084-4
Published by The Benjamin Company, Inc.
One Westchester Plaza
Elmsford, New York 10523
Printed in Singapore
9th Printing 1984

CONTENTS

Welcome to the exciting world of microwave cooking. You are joining the countless thousands of people who have discovered the joys of the microwave oven and have delighted in this fast, easy, and efficient method of cooking. But, as with any new appliance, before you start using it you should take time to read the instructions carefully. The illustrated introductory chapters will show and tell you all about the way the oven works, why it works that way, what it can do, and how to get the most out of it. There is nothing complicated about using the oven; all you need is a little understanding of the special qualities of microwave cooking and you'll be on your way. Like any comprehensive conventional cookbook, this book tries to leave nothing to chance, so that cooking in the microwave oven will be as easy as it looks, and is. Whether you plan to use the microwave for all of your cooking or only part of it, take a few minutes to familiarize yourself with the principles and techniques of the oven, then try the wonderful recipes in the chapters that follow. You'll soon find you'll never want to cook any other way but the microwave way.

To install your oven, follow the manufacturer's directions. A microwave oven operates on standard 110-120v household current and does not require an expert to ready it for regular use.

The microwave oven requires little maintenance. Again, follow your manufacturer's directions for the few simple cleaning steps. Unlike a conventional oven, which generates heat in the oven cavity, there is no heat in the microwave cavity, so food and grease do not bake on. No harsh cleaning agents or difficult cleaning tasks are necessary. Just a simple wiping is all you need to keep the oven clean.

Keep the door and gasket free of food buildup to maintain a tight seal. Now, let's find out how the microwave oven works.

How Does It Work?

In conventional cooking by gas or electricity, food on top of the stove cooks by heat applied to the bottom of the pan, and in the oven by hot air, which surrounds the food. In microwave cooking, microwaves travel directly to the food, without heating the oven. Inside the top of the microwave oven is a magnetron vacuum tube, which converts ordinary electrical energy into high-frequency microwaves, just like radio and television waves. A fan-like device called a stirrer helps distribute the microwaves evenly throughout the oven. Microwaves are waves of energy, not heat. They are either

← *Prime Rib Roast of Beef (Guide, page 69)*

reflected, pass through, or are absorbed, depending upon the material contacted. For example, metal reflects microwaves; glass, pottery, paper, and most plastics allow the waves to pass through; and, finally, food absorbs microwaves. Very simply then, the absorbed microwave energy causes the food molecules to vibrate rapidly against each other, inducing friction, which in turn produces the heat that cooks the food. This is somewhat like the way heat is generated when you rub your hands together. The waves penetrate the food, and cooking begins from the exterior. The interior then cooks by conduction. The prime rib photo on page 7 illustrates this principle. This process produces the much-appreciated cooking speed of the microwave oven. Because the cooking containers used in the microwave oven do not absorb microwave energy, they do not

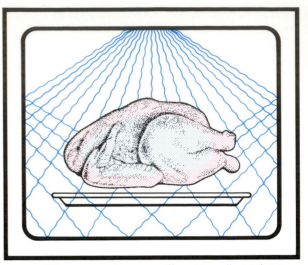

Microwaves bounce off oven walls and are absorbed by food. The air in the oven remains cool.

become hot. The microwaves pass through the containers directly into the food. However, the containers may absorb heat from the food itself, so you will occasionally need to use potholders. The see-through panel in the microwave oven door is made of a specially prepared material that contains a metal screen. The metal screen reflects the microwaves, yet enables you to observe the food as it cooks. The waves cannot penetrate this screen. Opening the microwave oven door turns the unit off automatically, so you can stir, turn, or check doneness with ease. And you don't have to face that blast of hot air you expect when opening a conventional oven.

Now that you've learned something about how the microwave oven works, let's take a look at all the wonderful things you can do with it.

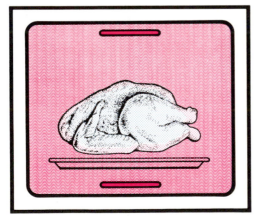

Conventional ovens cook by hot air.

You can cook just about anything in the microwave oven, but some foods are so especially good done this way that we want to show several of them to you. The recipes for all the dishes illustrated here are included in the book. You'll find that the microwave oven not only cooks food superbly from scratch, but also reheats and defrosts with excellent results. Let's take a look.

☐ *Roast beef* is juicy and rare, with less shrinkage than in the conventional oven. ☐ You can enjoy all kinds of *vegetables* at their wholesome best. Their true flavor and color are preserved. Potatoes are fluffy, cauliflower crisp, and broccoli the beautiful green it was born with. ☐ You'll want *scrambled eggs* for breakfast, lunch, and supper when you've tried them microwave-style. They're fluffier than in conventional cooking, and more pleasing to the eye as well as the palate. ☐ You'll think positively about *leftovers* after you try them reheated in the microwave. Food will have that just-cooked taste and look.

☐ Cook luscious *chocolate cakes,* so tantalizingly moist, rich, and high. ☐ *Fruit,* such as this baked apple, can be prepared without water; like vegetables, fruit retains that just-picked color and flavor. ☐ *Sauces* are a blessing to cook in the microwave oven. Constant stirring is a thing of the past. Just imagine the convenience of mixing, cooking, and serving all in the same container.

Hollandaise sauce is smooth with just a few stirrings. ☐ The microwave can't be beaten for *heating rolls and bread* so quickly they don't have a chance to be anything but perfect. And you can cook them right in the serving basket as long as there are no metal fasteners or trim. ☐ *Bacon* cooked in the microwave is incomparable — flat and crisp — and one slice takes less than a minute to

cook. It can be placed on a microproof bacon rack or between paper toweling. □ *Candy* is a particular favorite for microwave cooks because it's as easy as pie. Chocolate and caramelized mixtures won't require constant stirring. Try this white chocolate Almond Bark or the party mints and see for yourself. □ *Hot appetizers* are ready as needed, cooking quickly, with no mess and no pan to clean. Just cook them directly on paper plates or in a serving dish. Rumaki (bacon-wrapped chicken livers and water chestnuts) and mushrooms make delectable hors d'oeuvres. □ *Casseroles* cook without sticking and are just as good served later. This casserole is called Macaroni Supreme because it is!

□ Explore the pleasures of cooking *seafood* in your microwave oven. Fish fillets and steaks are moist and tender, their natural juices enhancing their delicate flavor. □ And for a pick-me-up that's really quick there's no equal to a *bowl of soup,* a cup of coffee, or a mug of cocoa served directly from the oven. □ *Melt chocolate* and *soften butter or cream cheese* in seconds and save the time and mess of double boilers and burned pans.

Now that you've had a sampling of what this appliance can do, let's take a look at what you need to know in order to start cooking.

In this chapter you will find everything you need to know to make microwave cooking easy, efficient, and pleasurable. Once you know the principles, the techniques will become second nature. Read this basic information with its accompanying illustrations carefully. As you begin to use the oven, you can always refer back to this handy guide whenever a question arises about a cooking term or method. Here you will learn why some foods cook faster than others, what you should know about timing and temperature, which cooking utensils are appropriate, how to cook most efficiently, and much more.

Because of the unique qualities of microwave energy, microwave cooking uses certain terms and methods that are different from those of conventional cooking. For example, in microwave cooking, many foods complete their cooking after being removed from the oven. This is known as standing time. In addition, how food is arranged in the cooking dish is important to its being cooked evenly throughout. You'll also discover the alternative method of microwave cooking with the automatic temperature probe. You'll be introduced as well to the oven's facility to defrost and to reheat quickly, with special hints for best results.

ABOUT TIMING

Time is an important element in microwave cooking. But isn't that statement true for all cooking? You, the cook, have to be the judge, as you consider your family's preferences and use your own instincts. Chances are, you can tell if a chicken is done simply by looking at it. You might even scoff at the timing chart given on a package because you know that a particular food always seems to need more or less time. It is important to know that even though the microwave oven is a superb product of computer technology, it is no more or less precise than any other cooking system. Nevertheless, because of the speed with which most foods are cooked, timing is more crucial in microwave cooking than in conventional cooking. One minute can cause a significant difference. When you consider that a cooking task requiring one hour in a conventional oven generally needs only one-quarter of that time in a microwave oven, you can understand why microwave cooking requires a somewhat different approach to timing. Where an extra minute in conventional cooking is seldom critical, in microwave cooking one minute can be the difference between overcooked and undercooked foods. As a result, most microwave recipes express probable minimum-maximum cooking times, as in "cook on 70 (roast) 4 to 5 minutes." This direction is often assisted by a phrase such as "or until sauce is thickened." As you become familiar with your oven you will recognize when to begin to check for doneness. Remember that it is better to under-cook and add more cooking time than to overcook — then it's too late.

Cooking times might be precise if a way could be found to guarantee that all foods would be exactly the same each time we cook them; if the utility company would guarantee not to alter our source of power (there are frequent changes in the voltage levels reaching our homes); and if the size, form, and content of foods would be consistently the same. The fact is that one potato or one steak varies from another in density, moisture or fat content, shape, weight, and temperature. This is true of all food.

The cook must be ready to adjust to the changes, to be flexible and observant. This discussion really comes down to the fact that you, not the microwave oven, are the cook. The oven can't make judgments, so you must. The recipes in this book have all been meticulously kitchen tested by expert home economists. You will find that the ranges of cooking times suggested are exact. As in all fine cooking, however, microwave cooking needs and benefits from your personal touch.

ABOUT FOOD CHARACTERISTICS

Food is made up of distinct elements that specifically affect timing in microwave cooking. Understanding these important qualities will help you become a skilled and successful microwave cook.

Quantity

The larger the volume of food there is, the more time is needed to cook it. For example, one potato may cook in 4 to 6 minutes but 2 potatoes take about one and a half times as long. One ear of corn in the husk cooks in about 3 minutes where 3 ears may cook in 8 minutes. Therefore, if the quantity in a recipe is changed, be sure to make an adjustment in timing. When increasing a recipe, increase the amount of cooking time. Here is a general rule to follow: When doubling a recipe, increase the cooking time approximately 50 percent. When cutting a recipe in half, reduce the time by approximately 40 percent.

Shape and Size

Thin food cooks faster than thick food; thin sections faster than thick. Small pieces also cook faster than large pieces. For even cooking, place thick pieces toward the outside of the dish since the outside areas cook faster than the inside areas. For best results, try to cook pieces of similar size and shape together.

of the oven. Food close to the top may require shielding with pieces of aluminum foil or turning for even cooking.

Density

Dense foods like potatoes, roast beef, and carrots take longer to cook than porous foods, such as cakes, ground

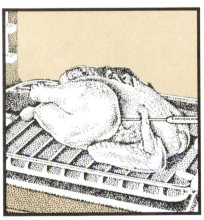

The density of food affects cooking time (above). Irregularly-shaped food requires special arrangement (above left). Food areas close to the energy source are turned or shielded during cooking (left).

Height

As in conventional cooking, areas that are closer to the energy source cook faster. In most microwave ovens, the energy source is at the top

beef, and apples, because it takes the microwaves longer to penetrate the denser texture. For example, a 2-pound roast will take longer than a 2-pound meat loaf.

Moisture Content

Moist food cooks faster than dry food because microwave energy is easily absorbed by the moisture within the food. For example, 1 cup of sliced zucchini will cook faster than 1 cup of carrots because of the high water content in the zucchini. In fact, the amount of free moisture within a food helps determine how rapidly it cooks.

Sugar and Fat Content

Food high in sugar and fat heats quicker than items low in these ingredients, because microwave energy is attracted by sugar and fat. For example, the fruit or cheese filling of a sweet roll will heat faster than the roll itself and will be hotter, since sugar and fat reach higher temperatures than food low in sugar or fat content.

Moist food cooks faster than dry (left). Frozen food takes longer to cook than canned (center). A sweet roll heats a bit faster than a dinner roll (right).

Delicate Ingredients

This term is used to refer to food that cooks so quickly in the microwave oven that it can overcook — toughening, separating, or curdling. For example, mayonnaise, cheese, eggs, cream, dairy sour cream, etc. Other food may "pop," such as snails, oysters, and chicken livers. For this reason, a lower power setting is often recommended for proper cooking. However, when these ingredients are mixed with other food, as in a casserole, stew, or soup, you may use a higher power setting, because volume automatically slows down the cooking.

Starting Temperature

As in conventional cooking, the temperature at which food is placed in the microwave oven affects the length of cooking time. More time is needed to cook food just out of the refrigerator than food at room temperature. For example, it takes longer to heat frozen green beans than canned green beans. Also, hot tap water will start boiling sooner than cold. Recipes in this book start with food at its normal storage temperature.

ABOUT UTENSILS

A wide variety of cookware and cooking implements can be used in the microwave oven. In order to indicate an item made of material that is safe and recommended for microwave cooking, we have created a new term, *microproof*. The Materials Checklist and Microproof Utensils Chart on the following pages will aid you in selecting the appropriate microproof utensil. Except for metal, most materials are microproof for at least a limited amount of cooking time. But unless specifically approved, items made of metal, even partially, are never to be used in the microwave oven, because they reflect microwaves, preventing them from passing through the cooking utensil into the food. In addition, metal that touches the oven sides will cause sparks, a static charge, known as arcing. Arcing is not harmful to you, though it will deface the oven. Metal twist ties or dishes or cups with gold or silver trim should not be used. See the Materials Checklist for those approved types of metal, such as pieces of aluminum foil, used as a shield over certain areas of food to prevent overcooking, or metal clips attached to frozen turkey.

When selecting a new piece of cookware, first check the manufacturer's directions. Also review the Materials Checklist and the Guide to Microproof Cookware. If you are still in doubt, try this test: Pour a cup of water into an ovenproof glass measure and place in the oven next to the container or dish to be tested.

Cook on HI (max. power) for 1 minute. If the new dish feels hot, don't use it — it is absorbing microwave energy. If it feels warm, the dish may only be used for warming food. If it remains at room temperature, it is *microproof.*

The rapid growth of microwave cooking has created many new products for use in the microwave oven. Among these are microproof replacements for cookware formerly available only in metal. You'll find a wide variety at your store — cake, bundt, and muffin pans, roasting racks, etc. When you add these to traditional microproof cookware and the incredible array of microproof plastic and paper products, you'll find that microwave cooking enables you to select from many more kinds of cookware than available for conventional cooking.

Selecting Containers

Containers should accommodate the food being cooked. Whenever possible use round or oval dishes, so that the microwaves are absorbed evenly into the food. Square corners in cookware receive more concentration of energy than the rest of the dish, so the food in the corners tends to overcook. Some cake and loaf recipes call for ring molds or bundt pans to facilitate more even cooking. This is because the center area in a round or oval dish generally cooks more slowly than the outside. Round cookware with a small glass inserted open end up in the center works just as well to eliminate undercooked centers. When a particular size or

Unique roasting racks, browning dishes, and other cookware have been developed for microwave use (top left). Familiar items, such as molds and muffin pans, are now available in microproof materials (top right). A wide variety of glass, ceramic, and wood items are perfect for microwave use (above right). All kinds of paper products make microwave cooking especially easy (above left). Many plastics are safe for microwave use (left).

shape of container is specified in a recipe, it should be used. Varying the container size or shape may change cooking time. A 2-quart casserole called for in a recipe refers to a bowl-shaped cooking utensil. A 12×8-inch or a 9-inch round baking dish refers to a shallow cooking dish. In the case of puddings, sauces, and candies, large containers are specified to prevent the liquids, especially milk-based ones, from boiling over. For best results, try to use the dish cited in the recipe.

Materials Checklist

☐ CHINA, POTTERY: Ideal for micro-wave use. However, if they have metallic trim or glaze, they are not microproof and should not be used.

☐ GLASS: An excellent microwave cooking material. Especially useful for baking pies to check doneness of pie shells through the bottom. Since ovenproof glass is always safe, "microproof" is not mentioned in any recipe where a glass item is specified.

☐ METALS: *Not* suitable except as follows:
  Small strips of aluminum foil can be used to cover areas on large pieces of meat or poultry that defrost or cook more rapidly than the rest of the piece — for example, a roast with jagged areas or thin ends, or the wing or breast bone of poultry. This method is known as shielding in microwave cooking.
  Shallow aluminum frozen TV dinner trays with foil covers removed can be heated, provided that the trays do not exceed 3/4 inch depth. (However, TV dinners heat much faster if you "pop" the blocks of food out and arrange them on microproof dinner plates.)
  Frozen poultry containing metal clamps may be defrosted in the microwave oven without removing the clamps. Remove the clamps after defrosting.
  Trays or any foil or metal item must be at least 1 inch from oven walls.

☐ PAPER: Approved for short-term cooking and for reheating at low settings. These must not be foil-lined. Extended use may cause the paper to burn. Waxed paper is a suitable covering.

☐ PLASTICS: May be used if dish-washer safe, but only for limited cooking periods or for heating. Do not use plastics for tomato-based food or food with high fat or high sugar content.

☐ PLASTIC COOKING POUCHES: Can be used. Slit the pouch so steam can escape.

☐ STRAW AND WOOD: Can be used for quick warming. Be certain no metal is used on the straw or wood items.

Browning Dish

A browning dish is used to sear, grill, fry, or brown food. It is made to absorb microwave energy when the dish is preheated empty. A special coating on the bottom of the dish becomes very hot when preheated in the microwave oven. There are a variety of dishes available. Follow the manufacturer's instructions for care and use and for the length of time to preheat the dish.

After the dish is preheated, vegetable oil or butter may be added to enhance the browning and prevent food from sticking. After the food is placed on the preheated browning dish, the dish is returned to the oven, where the microwaves cook the interior of the food while the hot surface of the dish browns the exterior. The food is then turned over to brown the other side. When cooking hamburger or moist foods, you may wish to pour off accumulated juices before turning the food over. The longer you wait to turn the food the less browning occurs, since the dish cools off rapidly. You may need to drain the dish, wipe it out, and preheat it again. In doubling a recipe, such as fried chicken, wipe out the browning dish after the first batch, reheat the empty dish, and repeat the procedure. Since the browning dish becomes very hot, be sure to use potholders when handling it.

Used as a grill, the browning dish speeds cooking time. However, if you wish to use the dish to brown certain foods prior to adding them to a recipe, your recipe time will remain about the same. Some foods, such as eggs or sandwiches, require less heat for browning than other foods, such as chicken or meat.

Bottom Glass Tray

The bottom glass tray in the microwave oven is the primary cooking level. It is made of glass because microwaves penetrate glass to cook the bottom of the food. Glass is also easy to clean. Never operate the oven without the bottom tray in place.

Middle Metal Rack

The removable middle metal rack of your oven is used mainly in whole-meal cooking or when certain double quantities are cooked. The rack is made of specially engineered metal and is safe for the microwave oven. The microwaves bounce off the rack and are absorbed by the food. Generally, for more even and faster cooking, it is best to cook a few batches one after another rather than on two levels at the same time. The rack should be removed from the oven when not in use.

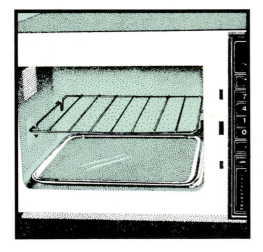

The bottom glass tray is the primary cooking level. The middle metal rack is used for whole meal cooking (page 183) and certain double-batch recipes such as Oysters Rockefeller (page 115).

A GUIDE TO MICROPROOF COOKWARE

ITEM	GOOD USE	GENERAL NOTES
China plates, cups	Heating dinners and drinks.	No metal trim.
Cooking pouches (plastic)	Cooking meat, vegetables, rice, other frozen food.	Slit pouch so steam can escape.
Corelle® Livingware	Heating dinners, soups, drinks.	Closed-handle cups should not be used.
Corning Ware® or Pyrex casseroles	Cooking main dishes, vegetables, desserts.	No metal trim.
Microwave browning dishes or grills	Searing, grilling, and frying small meat items; grilling sandwiches; frying eggs.	These utensils are specially made to absorb microwaves and preheat to high temperatures. They brown food that otherwise would not brown in a microwave oven.
Microwave roasting racks	Cooking roasts and chickens, squash and potatoes.	Special racks are available for cooking bacon.
Oven film and cooking bags	Cooking roasts or stews.	Substitute string for metal twist ties. Bag itself will not cause tenderizing. Do not use film with foil edges.
Paper plates, cups, napkins	Heating hot dogs, drinks, rolls, appetizers, sandwiches.	Absorbs moisture from baked goods and freshens them. Paper plates and cups with wax coatings should not be used.
Plastic wrap	Covering dishes.	Fold back edge to ventilate, allowing steam to escape.
Pottery and earthenware plates, mugs, etc.	Heating dinners, soups, drinks.	Some pottery has a metallic glaze. To check, use dish test (page 15).
Soft plastics, sherbet cartons	Reheating leftovers.	Used for very short reheating periods.
Thermometers	Measuring temperature of meat, poultry, and candy.	Use only approved microproof meat or candy thermometer in microwave oven. Microwave temperature probe is available with oven (see page 26).
TV dinner trays (aluminum)	Frozen dinners or homemade dinners.	No deeper than ¾ inch. Food will receive heat from top surface only. Foil covering food must be removed.
Waxed paper	Covering casseroles. Use as a tent.	Prevents splattering. Helps contain heat where a tight seal is not required Food temperature may cause some melting.
Wooden spoons, wooden skewers, straw baskets	Stirring puddings and sauces; for shish kabobs, appetizers, warming breads.	Can withstand microwaves for short cooking periods. Be sure no metal fittings on wood or straw.

ABOUT METHODS

The evenness and speed of microwave cooking are affected not only by the characteristics of the food itself, but also by certain methods, described below. Some of these techniques are used in conventional cooking as well, but they have a particular application in microwave cooking because of the special qualities of microwave energy. Many other important variables that in-

Arrangement

The way food is arranged in the dish and in the oven enhances even cooking and speeds defrosting and cooking. The microwaves penetrate the outer portion of food first; therefore, food should be arranged so that the denser, thicker areas are near the edge, and the thinner, more porous areas are near the center. For example, when cooking broccoli, split the heavy stalks to expose more

Microwave arrangement methods create unique cook-and-serve opportunities. The cauliflower and broccoli dish, for example, is cooked, covered, for 9 minutes on HI (max. power) with 1/4 cup water.

fluence cooking, defrosting, and reheating in the microwave oven are included here. Becoming familiar with these terms and methods will make microwave cooking easy and successful.

area, then overlap with flowerets; or you can alternate flowerets of cauliflower with broccoli for an attractive dish. This gives even density to the food and provides even cooking. Place shrimp in a ring with the tails toward the center. Chicken legs should be arranged like the spokes of a wheel, with the bony end toward the center. Food such as cupcakes, tomatoes, and potatoes should be arranged in a circle, rather than in rows.

throughout. When rearranging food, move the center food to the outside of the dish and the outer food toward the center. Such recipes as Tomato Swiss Steak (page 78), and Quick Brunswick Stew (page 98) call for rearranging.

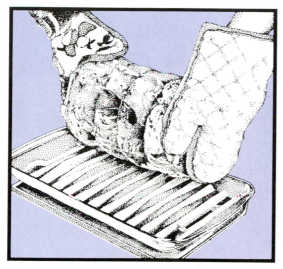

Turning Over

As in conventional cooking, some food, such as large roasts, whole poultry, a ham, or hamburgers, may require turning over to brown each side and to promote even heating. Any food seared on the browning dish should be turned over. During the defrosting process in the microwave oven, it is often necessary to turn the food.

Rearranging

Sometimes food that cannot be stirred needs repositioning in the cooking utensil to allow even heating

Stirring

Less stirring is required in microwave cooking than in conventional cooking. When necessary, stir from the outside to the center, since the outside heats faster than the center portion. Stirring blends the flavors and promotes even heating. Stir only as directed in the recipes. Constant stirring is never required in microwave cooking.

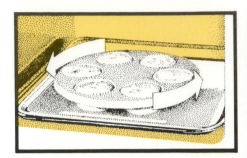

A one-quarter rotation is used for some muffins and cakes (above left). Covers are as important in microwave cooking as in conventional (left and above).

Rotating

A few foods, such as pies and cakes, that cannot be stirred, turned over, or rearranged call for repositioning the cooking dish one-quarter turn to allow· for even distribution of the microwave energy. Rotate only if the baked food is not cooking or rising evenly. Most food does not need to be rotated.

Covering

Covers are used to trap steam, prevent dehydration, speed cooking time, and help food retain its natural moisture. Suitable tight coverings are microproof casserole tops, glass covers, plastic wraps, oven bags, and microproof plates and saucers. Boilable freezer bags may be used as containers for the frozen food inside. Pierce top with a knife to ventilate before cooking. Remove coverings away from your face to prevent steam burns. Paper toweling is especially useful as a light covering to prevent splatter and to absorb moisture. Waxed paper helps retain heat and moisture.

Shielding

Certain thin or bony areas, such as the wing tips of poultry, the head and tail of fish, or the breastbone of a turkey, cook faster than thicker areas. Covering these parts with small pieces of aluminum foil shields these areas from overcooking, since aluminum foil reflects the waves. Besides preventing thin parts of food from cooking more rapidly than thicker ones, shielding may be used during defrosting to cover those portions that defrost more quickly than others. Use aluminum foil only when recommended in recipes. Be careful not to allow the foil to touch the oven walls.

Standing Time

This term refers to the time food needs to complete cooking or thawing after the microwave time has ended. During standing time, heat continues to be conducted from the outside to the center of the food. After the oven is turned off, food may remain in the oven for standing time or may be placed on a heatproof counter. This procedure is an essential part of food preparation with the microwave oven. Some food, such as roasts, requires standing time to attain the proper internal temperature for rare, medium, or well-done levels. Casseroles need standing time to allow the heat to spread evenly and to complete reheating or cooking. With cakes, pies, and quiches, standing time permits the center to finish cooking. During the standing time outside the oven, place food on a flat surface, such as a heat-resistant bread board or counter top, not on a cooling rack as you would conventionally.

Piercing

It is necessary to break the skin or membrane of certain food, such as egg yolks, potatoes, liver, chicken giblets, eggplant and squash. Because the skins or membranes retain moisture during cooking, they must be pierced before cooking to prevent bursting and to allow steam to escape. For example, pierce sausage casing in several places before cooking. A toothpick may be used for egg yolks; a fork is best for potatoes and squash; a knife is best to slit plastic cooking bags.

Piercing (above right). The effect of standing time on roast beef (right). Use a flat surface for standing time (above).

Browning

Many foods do not brown in the microwave oven as much as they do in the conventional oven. Depending upon the fat content, most food will brown in 8 to 10 minutes in the microwave oven. For example, bacon browns in minutes because of its high fat content, but poultry will not brown even after 10 minutes. For food that cooks too quickly to brown, such as hamburgers, fried eggs, steak or cutlets, a special browning dish is available (page 17). The longer the cooking time, or the higher the fat content, the more browning will be achieved. You can also create a browned look on roasts, poultry, steaks, and other foods by brushing on a browning agent, such as gravy mix, soy sauce, dehydrated onion soup mix, paprika, etc. Cakes, bread, and pie shells do not brown as they do in conventional cooking. Using chocolate, spices, or dark flour helps attain the dark color. Otherwise, you can create appealing color by adding frostings, toppings, or glazes.

Adjusting for High Altitudes

As in conventional cooking, microwave cooking at high altitudes requires adjustments in cooking time for leavened products like breads and cakes. Other food may require a slightly longer cooking time to become tender, since water boils at a lower temperature. Usually, for every 3 minutes of microwave cooking time you add 1 minute for the higher altitude. Therefore, a recipe calling for 3 minutes needs 4 minutes and a recipe requiring 6 minutes needs 8 minutes. The wisest procedure is to start with the time given in the recipe and then check for doneness before adding additional time. Adding time is easy, but overcooking can be a real problem. Here again your judgment is vital.

Programming

The microwave oven has a built-in computer. The computer accepts your instructions, called programming, and causes the oven to perform accordingly. Set the time or temperature, the cook control setting, and start. The oven will automatically turn off when the desired time or temperature is reached. Check your Use and Care Instructions for details.

Your microwave oven gives you the ability to select from many power settings in graduated form from zero to 100 percent — HI (max. power). Just as in a conventional oven, these settings give you flexibility and the necessary control to produce perfectly cooked dishes. You can set your multi-power oven to suit the food being cooked. Many foods require slow cooking at less than full power to achieve the best results. In addition to HI (max. power) there are 99 multi-power settings. Each recipe in the book indicates which power setting is recommended for the food being cooked. The following chart outlines the specific uses for the main settings.

Touch Pad

The touch pad on the oven control panel needs only to be touched to activate the oven. The beep tone sounds to assure you that the setting is being entered.

Guide for Cook Control Settings	
Main Setting	**Suggested Cooking Uses**
1	Raising bread dough
10 (warm)	Softening cream cheese; keeping casseroles and main dishes warm.
20 (low)	Softening chocolate; heating breads, rolls, pancakes, tacos, tortillas, and French toast; clarifying butter; taking chill out of fruit; heating small amounts of food.
30 (defrost)	Thawing meat, poultry,and seafood; finish cooking casseroles. stews. and some sauces: cooking small quantities of most food.
40 (braise)	Cooking less tender cuts of meat in liquid and slow cooking dishes; finish cooking less tender roasts.
50 (simmer)	Cooking stews and soups after bringing to a boil: cooking baked custards and pasta.
60 (bake)	Cooking scrambled eggs: cakes.
70 (roast)	Cooking rump roast, ham, veal, and lamb; cooking cheese dishes; cooking eggs,and milk; cooking quick breads and cereal products.
80 (reheat)	Quickly reheating precooked or prepared food: heating sandwiches.
90 (sauté)	Quickly cooking onions. celery. and green peppers: reheating meat slices quickly.
HI (max. power)	Cooking tender cuts of meat; cooking poultry, fish, vegetables, and most casseroles; preheating the browning dish: boiling water; thickening some sauces; cooking muffins. Cooking whole meal, i.e. two or three dishes at once (see pages 183-188).

Temperature Probe

When inserted into the food, this special feature of your microwave oven allows you to cook the food to a preselected internal temperature. When the desired temperature is reached the oven automatically turns off or keeps food warm if your particular model has that feature. Instead of setting the oven to an approximate number of minutes, you set the probe at the exact temperature that it should reach to attain desired doneness. The oven must also be set at the power level at which the food is to be heated. If a power level is not selected, the oven automatically remains at HI (max. power). The probe provides accuracy in cooking almost any food, from instant coffee and sauces to beef casseroles and roast chicken. You can even watch the display window as the food reaches its programmed temperature. If there is to be a delay in serving, don't worry; the oven has an automatic "hold warm" feature.

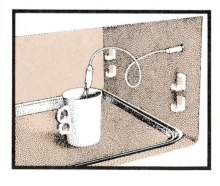

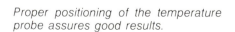

Proper positioning of the temperature probe assures good results.

Favorite Meatloaf (page 79) is easiest when the temperature probe is used.

The probe must be carefully and properly inserted in the food to obtain the best results. As a rule, the probe tip should be in the center of the dish, cup, or casserole or in the thickest portion of the meat. Do not allow the probe to touch bone, fat, or any metal foil if it is being used as a shield. After using the probe, remove from oven, use warm soapy water to wash the part that contacted the food, rinse, and dry. Do not immerse the entire unit in water or wash it in the dishwasher.

The "Guide to the Temperature Probe" provides a range from 120° to 200°F. Follow the directions in the recipes for placement of the probe, temperature, and covering of the dish, if specified, and consult the tips below for step-by-step directions for using the probe.

Standing time is essential for most foods to reach their optimum serving temperature. Because of the nature of microwave energy, during standing time the temperature of most food rises about 5° to 15°F. For example, after 10 minutes of standing time, the temperature of rare beef will reach 135°F; well done lamb will reach its proper 170° to 180°F. The temperature of beverages, however, drops in 10 minutes from 150° to 136°F.

Guide to the Temperature Probe*

Suggested Temperature Probe Settings	
120°	Rare Beef, Fully Cooked Ham
130°	Medium Beef
140°	Fish Steaks and Fillets, Well Done Beef
150°	Vegetables, Hot Drinks, Soups, Casseroles
155°	Veal
165°	Well Done Lamb, Well Done Pork
170°	Poultry Parts
180°	Well Done Whole Poultry
200°	Cake Frosting

* Refer to individual Cooking Guides (see Index) for specific instructions.

Tips for Probe Use

1. Place food in container, as recipe directs.
2. Place temperature probe in the food with the first inch of probe secured in the center of the food. Probe should not touch bone or a fat pocket. Probe should be inserted from the side or the front, not from the top of the food, except when inserting into casseroles, a cup of soup, etc. In general, try to insert probe as close to a horizontal position as possible.

3. Plug temperature probe into the receptacle on side wall of oven cavity.
4. Make sure the longer end of the temperature probe, inserted in the food, does not touch the bone, cooking container, or the sides of the oven.
5. Touch "Clear."
6. Touch "Temperature Control." Select temperature.
7. If a power setting other than HI (max. power) is desired, touch "Cook Control." Set power level.
8. Touch "Start."
9. Never operate the oven with the temperature probe in the cavity unless the probe is plugged in and inserted into the food or liquid.
10. Use potholders to remove temperature probe. It may be hot.
11. Do not use temperature probe with a browning dish or aluminum TV trays.

Reheating

One of the major assets of the microwave oven is its efficiency in reheating cooked food. Not only does most food reheat quickly, but it also retains moisture and its just-cooked flavor when properly arranged and covered. If someone is late for dinner, there's no need to fret. Just place a microproof plate containing the cooked food in your oven; in moments, dinner is ready once again. Reheat food in serving dishes or on paper plates and save extra clean-up time. Take-out food, which usually arrives at your home cooled off, can be easily reheated in seconds to its original state in your microwave oven. No more cold pizzas! Or lukewarm hamburgers. Leftovers are a treat too. You may even want to prepare food the day before, refrigerate, and serve the following day. You'll no longer call food leftovers, because it will taste as if "just made." Follow the tips below to help get excellent results when you are reheating food.

☐ Use 80 (reheat) except when otherwise specified. You can use the temperature probe for reheating casseroles, beverages, and other appropriate food. Insert probe into the largest or most dense piece of food and set temperature control at 150° to 160°F.

☐ To arrange a combination of different foods on a plate, place the dense food, like meat, at the outer edges and the more porous food, like breads, toward the center. Food that cooks most quickly should be placed at the center, with slower cooking food at the edges.

☐ Dense food, such as mashed potatoes and casseroles, cooks more quickly and evenly if a depression is made in the center, or if the food is shaped in a ring.

☐ To retain moisture during reheating, cover food with plastic wrap or a microproof lid. Wrap breads and sandwiches in paper toweling to absorb moisture and prevent sogginess. Use waxed paper to hold heat in and still allow steam to escape.

☐ Spread food out in a shallow container rather than piling it high, for quicker and more even heating.

☐ As a general guide to reheating a plate of food start with 1½ to 2 minutes, then check for doneness. If the plate on which the food is cooked feels warm the food is probably heated through, since its warmth has heated the

Defrosting

One of the great attractions of the microwave oven is its ability to defrost raw food or heat frozen cooked food. You need only to set the oven at 30 (defrost) for most food and observe the swiftness and ease of defrosting almost any food. The few exceptions are provided in the Defrosting Guides at the beginning of each chapter.

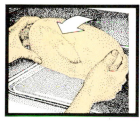

Defrost most food in its original wrapper (above left). Thawed portions of ground beef (above) are removed from the oven so cooking does not start. Fish fillets (far left) are separated as soon as possible. Many foods are turned over during defrosting (left).

plate. Because of the numerous variables in the food to be reheated, i.e., amount, shape, food characteristics, starting temperature, etc., recommended heating times can only be approximate.

Many of the same principles and techniques that apply to microwave cooking also apply to microwave defrosting and heating. Microwaves are attracted to water or moisture molecules. As soon as microwaves have defrosted a portion of the item they are more attracted to the thawed portion. The frozen portion continues to thaw, but this is due to the heat in the thawed portion. Special techniques, such as shielding and rotating, are helpful to be sure the thawed portion does not cook before the rest defrosts. It is often necessary to turn, stir, and separate to assist the defrosting process. Defrosting requires standing time to complete. Because food differs in size, weight, and density, recommended defrosting times can only be approximate. Additional standing time may be necessary to defrost completely. Read the Defrosting Guides throughout the book for times and special instructions about defrosting specific food. Here are some tips to aid you toward fast and easy defrosting:

☐ Poultry, seafood, fish, meat, and most vegetables may be defrosted in their original closed package. You may leave metal clips in poultry during defrosting, but you should remove them as soon as possible before cooking. Replace metal twists on bags with string or rubber bands before defrosting.

☐ Plastic-wrapped packages from the supermarket meat department may not be wrapped with a plastic wrap recommended for microwave use. If in doubt, unwrap package and place food on a microproof plate.

☐ Poultry wings, legs, and the small or bony ends of meat or fish may need to be covered with pieces of aluminum foil for part of the thawing time to prevent cooking while the remainder thaws.

☐ Large items should be turned and rotated halfway through defrosting time to provide more even thawing.

☐ Food textures influence thawing time. Because of air space, porous foods like cake and bread defrost more quickly than a solid mass, such as a sauce, or roast.

☐ Do not thaw food wrapped in aluminum or in foil dishes except as approved, page 17.

☐ The edges will begin cooking if meat, fish, and seafood are completely thawed in the microwave oven. Therefore, food should still be icy in the center when removed from oven. It will finish thawing while standing.

☐ Remove portions of ground meat as soon as thawed, returning frozen portions to the oven.

☐ To thaw half of a frozen vegetable package, wrap half the package with aluminum foil. When unwrapped side is thawed, separate and return balance to freezer.

☐ Thin or sliced items, such as fish fillets, meat patties, etc., should be separated as soon as possible. Remove thawed pieces and allow others to continue thawing.

☐ Casseroles, saucy foods, vegetables, and soups should be stirred once or twice during defrosting to redistribute heat.

☐ Frozen fried foods may be defrosted but will not be crisp when heated in the microwave oven.

☐ Freezing tips: It is helpful to freeze in small quantities rather than in one large piece. When freezing casseroles, it's a good idea to insert an empty paper cup in the center so no food is present there. This speeds thawing. Depressing the center of ground meat when freezing also hastens thawing later. Take care to wrap and package food well to retain its original quality. The wrapped food should be air-free, with air-tight seals. Store at 0°F. or less for no longer than the times recommended for freezing.

Now it's time for some practical experience using all the features of the microwave oven: first a quick hot drink, then a simple breakfast and, finally, an easy lunch. You have read through the preceding introductory material and have checked your Owner's Manual. Your oven is ready for use, so let's begin by making a cup of instant coffee, tea, or instant soup to enjoy right now!

Lesson One

A quick pick-me-up

Take your favorite mug or cup; be sure there is no gold or silver trim or metallic glaze. If you are not certain that your mug is microproof, test it as directed on page 15. Then follow these step-by-step directions:

1. Fill mug or cup with water and place in the center of the oven on the bottom glass tray. Close the oven door.

2. Touch the "clear" pad to clear any previous programming.

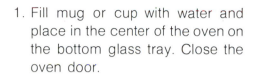

3. Touch the "time" pad and then touch pads 2-0-0. Your oven is now programmed to heat 2 minutes on HI (max. power). It is not necessary to touch "cook control" because your oven is automatically on HI (max. power) unless programmed to another setting.

4. Now touch the "start" pad.
5. The timer will beep when 2 minutes are up. The oven turns off automatically. Open the door.
6. Remove the mug. The handle will be cool enough to hold and the cup itself will be warm from the heated water.
7. Stir in instant coffee, tea, or instant soup.
8. Relax and have a nice "cuppa".

Lesson Two
Practice Breakfast

Frozen Orange Juice (5-ounce can)
Sweet Roll
Instant Coffee

1. Spoon frozen juice into a 4-cup glass measure or microproof serving pitcher, and place in oven. Close door.

8. Touch "clear" pad; touch "time" pad; then touch pads 3 and 0. Touch "cook control" pad, then pads 2 and 0. The oven is programmed for 30 seconds on 20 (low) setting.

2. Touch "clear" pad; touch "time" pad; then touch pads 2 and 0. The oven is programmed for 20 seconds at HI (max. power).

3. Touch "start."

4. When the timer beeps open door and remove container. Let stand 5 minutes before adding water.

5. Meanwhile, prepare coffee as directed on page 31.

6. Set sweet roll on paper plate or paper napkin.

7. Place in oven and close door.

9. Touch "start" pad. Bakery products should be only warm to the touch, since they will be hotter just below the surface. Because microwaves are attracted to sugar, the frosting or jelly may be very hot.

10. Enjoy your breakfast!

Lesson Three

Soup and Sandwich Lunch

1 cup soup (canned or homemade)
1 hot dog
1 hot dog bun, split

1. Pour soup into microproof serving cup.
2. Place tip of temperature probe in center of cup; plug other end into receptacle on side wall of oven cavity.
3. Close door.

4. Touch "clear," touch "temperature control," touch 1-5-0; touch "cook control," touch 8-0, touch "start." Your oven is now programmed to heat the soup to a temperature of 150° at a cook control setting of 80 (reheat).

5. Stir once during heating as follows: when display window shows 100°, open door; lift probe, stir soup, and replace probe. Close door and touch "start" again. The oven will continue to operate on the programming you set initially and will turn itself off when the soup reaches a temperature of 150°.
6. Remove temperature probe from oven after use.
7. Set soup aside, covered, while heating sandwich.
8. Place hot dog in bun, wrap in paper toweling. Set in oven and close door.

9. Touch "clear," "time," 5-0, "cook control," 8-0, and "start." Your oven is programmed to heat 50 seconds on 80 (reheat).
10. Bring the mustard; bon appetit!

By the Way . . .

To get the greatest pleasure out of your microwave oven, keep in mind that certain food is best done by conventional means of cooking. For the following reasons we don't recommend:

☐ Eggs cooked in the shell, because the light membrane surrounding the yolk collects energy, which then causes a steam build-up that will explode the egg. Don't experiment. It's a mess to clean up!

☐ Deep-fat frying, because the confined environment of the oven is not suited to the handling of the food or oil and is not safe.

☐ Pancakes, because no crust forms. (But the oven is great for reheating pancakes, waffles, and similar items.)

☐ Toasting, because it also requires crust development.

☐ Popovers, because of the slow steam development necessary to make them rise.

☐ Home canning, because it is impossible to judge exact boiling temperatures inside jar and you cannot be sure that the temperature and length of cook-ing are sufficient to prevent contamination of the food.

☐ Chiffon and angel food cakes, because they require steady, dry heat to rise and be tender.

☐ Heating bottles with small necks, like those for syrups and top-pings, because they are apt to break from the pressure build-up.

☐ Large items, such as a 25-pound turkey or a dozen baking potatoes, because the space is not adequate and no time is saved.

Finally, about popcorn:

Do not attempt to pop corn in a paper bag, since the corn may dehydrate and overheat, causing the paper bag to catch on fire. Due to the many variables, such as the age of the corn and its moisture content, popping corn in the microwave oven is not recommended. Microwave popping devices are available. While safe to use, they usually do not give results equal to those of conventional pop-ping methods. If the microwave device is used, *carefully follow the instructions provided with the product.*

You will undoubtedly want to cook some of your favorite conventional recipes in the microwave oven. With a little thought and experimenting you can convert many recipes. Before converting a recipe, study it to determine if it will adapt well to microwave cooking. Look for a recipe in the book that matches your conventional one most closely. For example, find a recipe with the same amount, type, and form of main ingredient, such as 1 pound ground meat or 2 pounds beef cut in 1-inch pieces, etc. Then compare other ingredients, such as pasta or vegetables. The microwave recipe will probably call for less liquid, because there is so little evaporation in microwave cooking. At the beginning of each recipe chapter hints on adapting recipes are provided. Also use the following guidelines:

- [ ] Candies, bar cookies, meatloaf, and certain baked goods may not need adjustments in ingredients. In puddings, cakes, sauces, gravies, and some casseroles, liquids should be reduced.

- [ ] Many casseroles will require adjustment in the order in which ingredients are added. Certain ingredients, such as uncooked rice, in a conventional recipe take longer to cook than others. When converting to the microwave, substitute a quicker-cooking ingredient, such as precooked rice.

For example, substitute instant onion flakes for chopped onion, and cut vegetable ingredients, such as carrots, in smaller pieces than the conventional recipe recommends.

- [ ] Most converted recipes will require adjustments in cooking time. Although a "rule of thumb" always has exceptions, you can generally assume that most microwave recipes are heated in about one-quarter to one-third of the conventional recipe time. Check for doneness after one-quarter of the time before continuing to cook.

Now let's try converting a conventional recipe to the microwave oven. Suppose you have a favorite recipe for Chicken Marengo that you would like to prepare in your microwave oven. The closest recipe in this book turns out to be Chicken Cacciatore (page 97). Let's see how to go about converting.

Chicken Marengo
Conventional Style
4 to 6 servings

½   cup flour
1   teaspoon salt
½   teaspoon pepper
1   teaspoon tarragon
1   chicken, 3 pounds, cut up
¼   cup olive oil
¼   cup butter
1   cup dry white wine
2   cups canned tomatoes
1   clove garlic, finely chopped
8   mushrooms (½ pound), sliced
    Chopped parsley

Preheat oven to 350° F. Mix flour, salt, pepper, and tarragon, and dredge chicken with seasoned flour. Reserve remaining flour.

In skillet heat oil and butter, and brown chicken. Place chicken in large casserole. Add reserved flour to the fat in skillet and, using a wire whisk, gradually stir in wine. When sauce is thickened and smooth, pour over the chicken and add the tomatoes, garlic, and mushrooms. Cover casserole and bake until chicken is tender, about 45 minutes. Before serving sprinkle with parsley.

Checking the Chicken Cacciatore recipe, you'll notice that the amount of liquid is quite a bit less than in the conventional Chicken Marengo recipe. That's because liquids do not reduce in microwave cooking and we don't want a thin sauce. Notice, too, that the onion is cooked first to be sure it is tender and that the flavor of the dish is fully developed. In converting, the Chicken Marengo recipe has the liquid reduced and the garlic is cooked first. Since the volume of food is about the same, the cooking times and power settings for Chicken Cacciatore are followed for Chicken Marengo Microwave Style. Here's the fully converted recipe:

Chicken Marengo
Microwave Style
4 to 6 servings

1   chicken, 3 pounds, cut up
1   teaspoon salt
½   teaspoon pepper
1   teaspoon tarragon
1   clove garlic, minced
1   tablespoon butter
1   tablespoon olive oil
¼   cup flour
½   cup dry white wine
2   cups canned tomatoes
8   mushrooms (½ pound), sliced
    Chopped parsley

Rub chicken with salt, pepper, and tarragon and set aside. Place garlic, butter, and olive oil in 3-quart microproof casserole. Cook, covered, on HI (max. power) 1 minute. Add flour, stir until smooth, gradually adding wine. Stir in tomatoes and mushrooms. Cook, covered, on HI (max. power) 5 minutes, stir. Add chicken, immersing pieces in sauce. Cook, covered, on HI (max. power) 25 to 30 minutes, or until chicken is fork tender. Taste for seasoning, sprinkle with chopped parsley, and allow to stand covered 5 minutes before serving.

Butter, olive oil, and flour have been reduced since browning is not part of the microwave recipe. If you wish, however, add more butter and olive oil, dredge chicken in flour, and brown chicken in preheated browning dish. The white wine has been reduced to avoid a too thin sauce.

Cooking Casseroles

The microwave oven is exceptionally good for cooking casseroles. Vegetables keep their bright fresh color and crisp texture. Meats are tender and flavorful. Here are some general hints to help you:

☐ Most casseroles can be made ahead of time, refrigerated or frozen, then reheated later in the microwave.

☐ Casseroles are usually covered with plastic wrap or glass lids during cooking.

☐ Allow casseroles to stand 5 to 10 minutes before serving, according to size. Standing time allows the center of the casserole to complete cooking.

☐ You will obtain best results if you make ingredients uniform in size, stirring occasionally to distribute heat. If the ingredients are of different sizes, stir more often.

☐ Casseroles containing less tender meat need longer simmering on a lower power setting, such as 40 (braise) or 50 (simmer). Casseroles with delicate ingredients such as cream or cheese sauces often need a lower setting like 70 (roast). Cheese toppings added for the last 1 or 2 minutes should cook at a setting no higher than 70 (roast).

☐ When used in quick-cooking casseroles, celery, onions, green peppers, and carrots should be sautéed before being added to dish. Rice or noodles should be partially cooked before combining with cooked meat, fish, or poultry. Use higher power settings, such as 80 (reheat) or HI (max. power), for these recipes.

About Low Calories

Scattered through the book are low-calorie suggestions and low-calorie recipes. They are listed in the index so you can find them when you need them. In general, you can lower calories in many recipes by making substitutions such as these:

Bouillon or water for butter when sautéing or softening vegetables
Vegetables for potatoes or pasta
Lean meats for fatty ones
Skim milk for whole milk
Skim milk cheeses like low-fat cottage, ricotta, and mozzarella for creamy fatty ones
Natural gravy with herbs for cream and butter sauces (you can stir yogurt in during final step)
Fruit cooked in its natural juices for those cooked with sugar added
Skinless chicken breast for regular cut-up chicken
Shellfish, and white fish such as sole, halibut, and flounder for mackerel, tuna, and other oily fish

Appetizers can be the most creative food of today's entertaining. They can be hot or cold, simple or fancy, light or hearty depending upon the occasion. There are no rules, so you can let your imagination soar. Until now *hot* appetizers were the most troublesome and time-consuming for the host or hostess. But that's no longer true with the microwave oven. Parties are much easier and more enjoyable because the microwave eliminates all that last-minute hassle and lengthy cooking over a hot stove. You can assemble most appetizers and nibbles in advance, and at the right moment, just coolly "heat 'n serve!" This chapter presents many recipes for entertaining your guests, but you'll also be tempted to prepare delicious snacks and munchies just for the family. There's no doubt about it — appetizers cooked in the microwave oven are fun to make, fun to serve, and fun to eat.

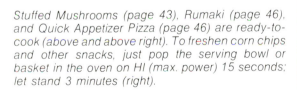

Stuffed Mushrooms (page 43), Rumaki (page 46), and Quick Appetizer Pizza (page 46) are ready-to-cook (above and above right). To freshen corn chips and other snacks, just pop the serving bowl or basket in the oven on HI (max. power) 15 seconds; let stand 3 minutes (right).

← *Shrimp and Artichokes (page 41), Tiny Meatballs (page 41), Toasted Seasoned Pecans (page 41), Nachos (page 42)*

Converting Your Own Recipes

Most of the hot appetizers you've always wanted to make will adapt well to microwave cooking, except for those wrapped in pastry, since the coating does not become crisp. The recipe for Rumaki is an ideal guide for countless skewered appetizers containing seafood, chicken, vegetable, and fruit combinations. And compare your favorite dip recipe with one of the choices here to determine your microwave time and power setting. The enormous variety of finger foods, dippings, and canapés will provide you with continual tasty surprises. Here are some helpful tips:

☐ Appetizers and dips that contain cheese, mayonnaise, and other such delicate ingredients are usually heated on 70 (roast). A higher setting might cause separation or drying.

☐ The temperature probe set at 130°F. on 70 (roast) provides an excellent alternative for heating hot dips containing seafood, cheese, or foods to be served in a chafing dish or fondue pot.

☐ Because of its very delicate nature, a sour cream dip should be covered and heated with the temperature probe to 90° on 50 (simmer).

☐ Toppings for canapés can be made ahead, but do not place on bread or crackers until just before heating to assure a crisp base.

☐ Cover appetizers or dips only when the recipe specifies doing so. Use fitted glass lids, waxed paper, plastic wrap, or paper toweling.

☐ You can heat two batches of the same or similar appetizers at one time by using both oven levels, the middle metal rack and bottom glass tray, for almost double the time of one batch. Watch closely; those on top may cook more quickly than those on bottom.

COOKING GUIDE — CONVENIENCE APPETIZERS

Food	Amount	Cook Control Setting	Time	or	Temperature Probe Setting	Special Notes
Canned meat spread	4 oz.	80 (reheat)	30-45 seconds			Transfer to small microproof bowl.
Canned sausages, cocktail sausages	5 oz.	80 (reheat)	1½-2 minutes			Place in covered glass casserole.
Cocktail franks, pizza roll	4 servings	70 (roast)	45-60 seconds			Place on paper towels. Roll will not crisp.
Cooked pizza, 10 inches, cut in 8 portions	1 wedge	80 (reheat)	45-60 seconds			Place on paper towels or paper plate or leave in uncovered cardboard box, points toward center.
	4 wedges	80 (reheat)	1½-2 minutes			
	Whole	70 (roast)	3¼-4 minutes			
Dips, cream	½ cup	10 (warm)	1½-2½ minutes	or	130°	Cover with plastic wrap.
Eggrolls, pastry-covered	2 servings	70 (roast)	30-45 seconds			Place on paper towels, do not cover.
Swiss fondue, frozen	10 oz.	80 (reheat)	5-6 minutes	or	150°	Slit pouch. Place on microproof plate. Stir before serving.

Shrimp and Artichokes
Total Cooking Time: 5 to 7 minutes

Arrange shrimp in single layer on flat, round microproof plate with shrimp tails toward the center. Cook, covered with waxed paper, on 70 (roast) 3 to 4 minutes. Remove shrimp as they become pink. Let stand about 5 minutes, then shell and devein. In microproof bowl, combine all remaining ingredients; cook, covered, on HI (max. power) 2 to 3 minutes, or until hot. Carefully stir in shrimp. Serve warm in chafing dish, with toothpicks.

about 36 pieces

1 pound small-sized raw shrimp, in shell
2 tablespoons olive oil
2 cloves garlic, minced
½ teaspoon salt
⅛ teaspoon pepper
½ teaspoon crumbled oregano
4 tablespoons lemon juice
½ teaspoon dill weed
1 jar (6 ounces) marinated artichokes hearts, drained
½ pound small fresh mushrooms

Tiny Meatballs
Total Cooking Time: 10 to 12 minutes

In large mixing bowl, combine ingredients and blend well. Form into small balls, about 1 inch in diameter. Arrange half the meatballs in a single layer in a microproof baking dish. Cook, uncovered, on 90 (sauté) 5 to 6 minutes. Place in chafing dish to keep hot. Cook remaining meatballs and add to chafing dish. Serve hot. Use toothpicks to spear meatballs and dunk in Curry Dipper (page 44). These may be prepared in advance and reheated just before serving on HI (max. power) 2 to 3 minutes.

about 60 meatballs

1 pound lean ground beef
½ pound ground pork
1 small onion, finely minced
1 cup milk
1 egg, lightly beaten
1 cup dry bread crumbs
1 teaspoon salt
¼ teaspoon pepper
¼ teaspoon ground allspice
2 teaspoons soy sauce

Toasted Seasoned Pecans
Total Cooking Time: 5 to 6 minutes

Place pecans in 1½-quart microproof casserole. Sprinkle with seasoned salt. Cut butter in 8 pieces and space evenly on top of pecans. Cook, uncovered, on HI (max. power) 5 to 6 minutes, stirring once or twice during cooking to distribute butter.

1 pound

1 pound pecan halves
1 tablespoon seasoned salt
¼ cup butter or margarine

You can make your own seasoned salt with garlic powder, paprika, cayenne, or curry powder. And you can use walnuts, cashews, almonds, or mixed nuts. Try your own combinations! For half the amount cut ingredients and cooking time in half. (We don't recommend roasting nuts in a shell.)

Nachos
Total Cooking Time: 1½ minutes

1 can (3⅛ ounces)
    jalapeño bean dip
1 bag (8 ounces) tortilla
    chips
1½ cups grated Cheddar cheese
1 can (2¼ ounces)
    jalapeño peppers

Spread bean dip lightly on tortilla chips. Top with cheese and the jalapeño peppers. Place 10 chips at a time on paper plate. Cook on 70 (roast) 30 seconds, or until cheese begins to melt. Serve hot.

30 canapés

This is one of those "do it now" recipes. Be sure to spread the dip on the chips just before cooking or you might end up with soggy chips.

Crunchy Chicken Wings
Total Cooking Time: 15 to 16 minutes

3 pounds chicken wings
¼ cup butter or margarine
18 buttery crackers
½ cup grated Parmesan cheese
2 teaspoons parsley flakes
½ teaspoon garlic powder
½ teaspoon paprika
    Dash pepper

Cut chicken wings apart at both joints; discard tips. Pat dry with paper towels. In 9-inch glass pie plate, melt butter on HI (max. power) 1 minute. Break crackers into blender, add remaining ingredients, and blend until crackers are crumbed and seasonings are mixed. Dip chicken in butter, then in seasoned crumbs. In pie plate, arrange chicken in spoke fashion with thicker part toward outside. Cook covered with paper towels on HI (max. power) 14 to 15 minutes, or until done. Serve hot.

28 pieces

You will delight your guests when you serve these as finger food at your next cocktail party. Be sure to provide lots of napkins!

Crab Supremes
Total Cooking Time: 1 to 1½ minutes

1 can (6½ to 7 ounces)
    crabmeat, drained
½ cup finely minced celery
2 teaspoons prepared mustard
4 teaspoons sweet pickle
    relish
2 green onions, thinly sliced
½ cup mayonnaise
16 crisp crackers or toast
    rounds

Pick over crabmeat and remove any cartilage. Place in 1-quart bowl and flake with fork. Add celery, mustard, pickle relish, green onions, and mayonnaise. Mix well. Spread mixture on crackers or toast rounds. Place 8 at a time on microproof plate lined with paper towels. Cover with waxed paper. Cook on 70 (roast) 30 to 45 seconds, or until hot. Repeat with remaining canapés.

16 canapés

Stuffed Mushrooms

Total Cooking Time: 7 to 9 minutes

Wash and dry mushrooms, remove stems. Chop stems, set aside. In 4-cup glass measure, combine bacon, green pepper, and onion. Cover with paper towels and cook on HI (max. power) 4 minutes, stirring once. Drain off fat. Add salt, cream cheese, Worcestershire, and mushroom stems. Mix well. Fill mushrooms with bacon mixture. In 2-cup glass measure, mix butter, bread crumbs, and parsley. Cook on HI (max. power) 1 minute. Press bread crumbs into top of bacon mixture. Place half the mushrooms on 9-inch microproof baking dish, stuffing side up. Cook on HI (max. power) 1 to 2 minutes. Repeat with remaining mushrooms.

about 50 mushrooms

1 pound small fresh mushrooms
4 slices bacon, diced
2 tablespoons minced green pepper
¼ cup minced onion
½ teaspoon salt
1 package (3 ounces) cream cheese
¼ teaspoon Worcestershire sauce
1 tablespoon butter or margarine
½ cup soft bread crumbs
1 teaspoon chopped fresh parsley

Cheddar Cheese Canapés

Total Cooking Time: 30 seconds

Combine Cheddar cheese, cream, Parmesan cheese, Worcestershire, hot-pepper sauce, and sesame seeds. Stir well until smooth. Spread 1 teaspoon of mixture on each toast round or cracker. Arrange 12 canapés on microproof platter. Cook on 70 (roast) 30 seconds, or until mixture is warm and cheese has melted. Repeat with remaining canapés. Garnish with parsley; serve warm.

12 canapés

   cup grated Cheddar cheese
2 tablespoons light cream
1 tablespoon grated Parmesan cheese
⅛ teaspoon Worcestershire sauce
⅛ teaspoon hot-pepper sauce
1 tablespoon sesame seeds
12 crisp crackers or toast rounds
   Chopped parsley

Party Nibblers

Total Cooking Time: 6½ to 7½ minutes

Mix pretzels, nuts, and cereal in large (12×8-inch) baking dish. Melt butter on HI (max. power) 1½ minutes. Stir in seasonings and Worcestershire. Drizzle over cereal; mix thoroughly. Cook on HI (max. power) 5 to 6 minutes, stirring after 3 minutes, or until evenly toasted. Cool and store in airtight container.

2½ quarts

Change combinations or add seasonings according to your taste.

2 cups thin pretzels
1 can (6 ounces) salted nuts (1½ cups)
2 cups crisp rice squares
2 cups crisp wheat squares
2 cups crisp oat circles
7 tablespoons butter or margarine
½ teaspoon garlic powder
½ teaspoon onion powder
½ teaspoon celery salt
1 teaspoon Worcestershire sauce

Liver and Sausage Paté
Total Cooking Time: 9 to 10 minutes

1 pound chicken livers
½ pound mild Italian sausages
⅓ cup cubed onion
1 tablespoon bourbon
¼ cup heavy cream
½ teaspoon salt
¼ teaspoon nutmeg

Butter a 7½ × 3¾ × 2½-inch loaf pan. Line buttered bottom and sides with waxed paper or aluminum foil. Rinse chicken livers under cold water, pat dry. Remove casing from sausages and break up meat. Place sausages in 4-cup glass measure. Cover with waxed paper and cook on HI (max. power) 4 minutes, or until sausages lose pinkness. Remove sausages from glass measure and set aside, reserving drippings. Pierce each chicken liver with toothpick to break the membrane. Place in glass measure with sausage drippings. Cook, covered, on HI (max. power) 3 to 4 minutes, or until livers lose pinkness. Stir once during cooking. Purée onion and bourbon in electric blender. Add livers and sausages, heavy cream, and seasonings. Cover and blend on high speed. Stop blender and push ingredients toward blades if necessary. Pour into prepared loaf pan and refrigerate 12 hours or overnight. Unmold and add topping about 2 hours before serving. Garnish with pimiento, capers, watercress, and green onions, if desired.

Topping:

2 packages (one 8 ounces and one 3 ounces) cream cheese
2 tablespoons butter or margarine
1½ tablespoons light cream

To prepare topping: soften together cream cheese and butter by removing foil wrap. Place on microproof plate, cook on 50 (simmer) 2 minutes. Place softened cream cheese and butter with cream in electric blender. Cover and blend on high until smooth and fluffy. Loosen paté and turn out onto serving platter. Carefully remove waxed paper or aluminum foil. Cover top and sides generously with cream cheese mixture. Refrigerate 1½ hours, or until cheese is firm. Let stand about 30 minutes at room temperature before serving. Serve with assorted crackers.

30 servings

Curry Dipper
Total Cooking Time: 2 minutes

1 can (10¾ ounces) cream of mushroom soup, undiluted
1½ tablespoons curry powder
1 clove garlic, minced
1 teaspoon lemon juice

In 4-cup glass measure, stir all ingredients together until well mixed. Cook on HI (max. power) 2 minutes, or until hot. Serve hot with Tiny Meatballs (page 41), cubed sirloin, shrimp, or scallops.

1¼ cups

Liver and Sausage Pâté, Stuffed Mushrooms (page 43) →

Cold Eggplant Appetizer

Total Cooking Time: 7½ to 9 minutes

1 eggplant (1 pound)
1 small onion, minced
½ medium green pepper, minced
1 clove garlic, minced
1 teaspoon lemon juice
½ teaspoon salt
⅛ teaspoon pepper
1 cup plain yogurt

Place whole eggplant on microproof baking rack, pierce skin in several places. Cook on HI (max. power) 6 to 7 minutes, or until soft. Set aside to cool. Combine onion, green pepper, garlic, and lemon juice in small microproof bowl. Cook on HI (max. power) 1½ to 2 minutes, or until vegetables are limp. Cut eggplant in half and scoop pulp into small mixing bowl. Add all ingredients except yogurt. Beat until well blended. Stir in yogurt, cover, and chill thoroughly before serving.

2 cups

Serve with pumpernickel or black bread, party rye or crackers. Cold eggplant is a wonderful low-calorie appetizer. If you serve it with cut-up raw vegetables instead of bread it is even lower in calories.

Rumaki

Total Cooking Time: 21 minutes

12 slices bacon
8 ounces chicken livers
¼ teaspoon garlic powder
¼ cup soy sauce
1 can (8 ounces) sliced water chestnuts, drained

Cut bacon slices in thirds and chicken livers in 1-inch pieces. Mix garlic powder in soy sauce. Dip chicken livers in soy sauce. Place 1 slice water chestnut on 1 piece liver and wrap in 1 slice bacon. Roll, secure, and fasten with wooden toothpick. Place 12 at a time in a circle on paper towel-lined microproof plate; cover with paper towels. Cook on HI (max. power) 4 minutes. Turn over, cover, and cook on HI (max. power) 3 minutes, or until bacon is cooked. Allow to stand 1 minute before serving.

36 appetizers

Quick Appetizer Pizza

Total Cooking Time: 9 to 12 minutes

6 English muffins, split and toasted
1 can (8 ounces) pizza sauce
1 package (4 ounces) pepperoni, sliced
1 cup shredded mozzarella cheese

Spread each toasted muffin half with pizza sauce. Top with 3 slices pepperoni and then with cheese. Place 4 halves on microproof serving plate in circle. Cook on 70 (roast) 3 to 4 minutes, or until cheese is melted. Let stand 3 minutes before serving. Repeat with remaining muffins.

12 servings

Microwaves perform at their very best with sandwiches, hot drinks, soups, and chowders. For a quick pick-me-up all you need is a minute or two and a mug full of water for a cup of instant soup, or coffee. And, if you like to make soups from scratch without those endless hours of simmering and hovering that are required by conventional cooking, follow these microwave recipes.

Rise and shine with breakfast cocoa and wind down your day with after-dinner coffee swiftly and easily made in your microwave oven. What a convenience for coffee lovers! No more of that bitter mess when coffee is kept warm for more than 15 minutes in the conventional way. Brew your coffee as you normally do and pour what you want to drink now. Refrigerate the rest. Then, throughout the day, pour single cups as you wish from the refrigerated pot. Heat for 1½ to 2 minutes on HI (max. power) and savor the taste of truly fresh coffee.

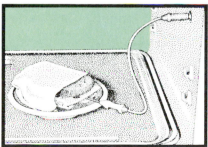

The temperature probe is especially helpful when preparing soup. Note the probe position when a bowl or casserole is covered with plastic wrap: the wrap is not pierced by the probe (above left). The temperature probe can be used when heating 1 to 4 cups of soup: arrange in a circle and insert the probe in one cup (above). Hot Ham and Swiss (page 57) is quickly heated using the probe (left).

Converting Your Own Soup and Hot Drink Recipes

Soups and hot drinks convert well and easily to the microwave method. Find a recipe here with the approximate density and volume of the family favorite or the new conventional recipe you want to try. You may have to alter an ingredient or two: for example, dried bean soups such as split pea and navy bean do not obtain the best results in microwave cooking. However, canned, precooked navy beans, kidney beans, and packaged dry soup mixes are perfect substitutes for dried beans and peas. The tips below will help you obtain excellent results with your own recipes:

☐ Be careful with milk-based liquids or 2- or 3-quart quantities, which can boil over quickly. Always select a large enough microproof container to prevent any boiling over, and fill individual cups no more than two-thirds full.

☐ Soup is cooked covered. Use microproof casserole lids, waxed paper, or plastic wrap.

☐ Soup with uncooked meat and chicken needs slower simmering. Start cooking on HI (max. power) and finish cooking on 50 (simmer). Generally, use 80 (reheat) for soups containing cooked meats and/or vegetables.

☐ Cooking time varies with the volume of liquid and density of food in soup.

☐ Remember that the microwave's brief cooking time results in less evaporation of liquid than stovetop simmering.

☐ Start with one-quarter the time recommended in a conventional recipe and adjust as needed to complete cooking.

Using the Hot Drinks Cooking Guide

1. Pour liquid into microproof cup.
2. The temperature of the liquid before heating will make a difference in final heating time. Water from the cold tap or milk from the refrigerator will take longer to heat.
3. Cook water-based drinks on HI (max. power). Heat milk-based drinks on 70 (roast), and watch carefully that they do not boil over.
4. Temperature probe may be used. Set at 150°F. Cook water-based drinks on HI (max. power) and milk-based drinks on 70 (roast).

COOKING GUIDE — HOT DRINKS

Liquid	Cook Control Setting	6-ounce Cup	Time (in minutes)	8-ounce Cup	Time (in minutes)	Special Notes
Water	HI (max. power)	1 2	1 to 1¼ 1¾ to 2	1 2	1½ to 2 3 to 3¼	For instant coffee, soup, tea, etc.
Milk	70 (roast)	1 2	2½ 2¾ to 3	1 2	2¾ to 3 3¼ to 3½	For cocoa, etc.
Reheating coffee	HI (max. power)	1 2	1 to 1½ 2 to 2¼	1 2	1¼ to 1½ 2 to 2½	

Using the Canned Soups Cooking Guide

1. Pour soup into 1½- or 2-quart microproof casserole.
2. Add milk or water as directed on can. Stir.
3. Cover with casserole lid, waxed paper, or plastic wrap.
4. Cook according to directions in Guide. Stir cream-style soups halfway through cooking times.
5. Temperature probe may be used. Set and cook as directed in Guide.
6. Let stand, covered, 3 minutes before serving.

COOKING GUIDE — CANNED SOUPS

Soup	Amount	Cook Control Setting	Time (in minutes)	or	Temperature Probe Setting	Special Notes
Broth	10¾ oz.	80 (reheat)	3½ - 4	or	150°	Use 1½-quart casserole
Cream Style:	10¾ oz.	80 (reheat)	5 - 6	or	140°	Use 1½-quart casserole
Tomato	26 oz.	80 (reheat)	8 - 10	or	140°	Use 2-quart casserole
Bean, Pea, or Mushroom	10¾ oz.	70 (roast)	7 - 8	or	150°	Use 1½-quart casserole
Undiluted chunk-style vegetable:	10¾ oz.	80 (reheat)	2½ - 4	or	150°	Use 1-quart casserole
	19 oz.	80 (reheat)	5 - 7	or	150°	Use 1½-quart casserole

Using the Quick Soup Cooking Guide

1. Pour water in microproof mug or casserole.
2. Cover with waxed paper or casserole lid.
3. Cook according to directions in Guide.
4. Let stand 5 minutes before serving.
5. Check noodles or rice, if any. If not cooked, return to oven at 80 (reheat) for 30 seconds.
6. Temperature probe may be used. Set as directed in Guide, cook on HI (max. power), and let stand 5 minutes before serving.

COOKING GUIDE — QUICK SOUPS

Soup	Number of Envelopes	Cook Control Setting	Time (in minutes)	or	Temperature Probe Setting	Special Notes
Instant soup 1¼-ounce envelope	1	HI (max. power)	2 - 2½	or	150°	Use 2/3 cup water in 8-ounce mug.
	2	HI (max. power)	3 - 3½	or	150°	Use 2/3 cup water per 8-ounce mug.
	4	HI (max. power)	6 - 7	or	150°	Use 2/3 cup water per 8-ounce mug.
Soup mix 2¾-ounce envelope	1	HI (max. power)	8 - 10	or	160°	Use 4 cups water in 2-quart casserole.

Converting Your Own Sandwich Recipes

The enormous variety of sandwich combinations you can heat in your microwave oven will tickle your imagination, and they are so easy to do. Combine meat and cheeses, eggs, salads, and vegetables; make "Dagwoods" or elegant tea sandwiches; and, of course, you'll want to cook the old standbys, hot dogs and hamburgers. Sandwiches heat in seconds, so be careful not to overcook — the bread can become tough and chewy. Heat breads until warm, not hot, and cheese just until it begins to melt. You can warm meat sandwiches, filled only with several thin slices of meat per sandwich, on HI (max. power) as follows:

1 sandwich   45 to 50 seconds
2 sandwiches 1 to 1½ minutes
4 sandwiches 2 to 2½ minutes

Follow these tips when adapting or creating your own sandwiches:

☐ The best breads to use for warmed sandwiches are day-old, full-bodied breads such as rye and whole wheat, and breads rich in eggs and shortening, like French or Italian and other white breads.
☐ Heat sandwiches on paper napkins, paper towels, or paper plates to absorb the steam and prevent sogginess. Cover with a paper towel to prevent splattering. More simply, you can wrap each sandwich in a paper towel. Remove wrapping immediately after warming.
☐ Thin slices of meat heat more quickly and taste better than one thick slice. The slower-cooking thick slice often causes bread to overcook before meat is hot.
☐ Moist fillings, such as that in a Sloppy Joe or a barbecued beef sandwich, should generally be heated separately from the rolls, to prevent sogginess.
☐ The browning dish can be used to enhance your grilled cheese, Reuben, or bacon sandwich. Brown the buttered outer side of bread before inserting filling.

Chilled Minted Pea Soup
Total Cooking Time: 7 to 10 minutes

¼ cup lightly packed fresh
     parsley, stems removed
2 green onions
½ medium head lettuce, cored
2 cups fresh peas or
     10-ounce package
     frozen peas
1 can (13¾ ounces)
     chicken broth
½ teaspoon salt
¼ cup coarsely chopped
     fresh mint leaves
¼ teaspoon white pepper
½ cup heavy cream
4 sprigs fresh mint for
     garnish

Chop parsley, green onions, and lettuce. Transfer to 2-quart casserole, add peas, chicken broth, salt, mint, and pepper. Cook on HI (max. power) 7 to 10 minutes, or until vegetables are tender. Pour the soup into a blender, cover, start at low speed and move to high until smooth. Stir in cream and cover. Chill until serving time. Garnish with mint.

4 servings

If fresh mint is not available, substitute 1 tablespoon dried mint leaves. Or, for an interesting variation, substitute ½ teaspoon dried thyme.

French Onion Soup

Total Cooking Time: 23 to 29 minutes

In 3-quart microproof casserole, cook onions and butter on HI (max. power) 10 to 12 minutes, or until onions are transparent, stirring once during cooking. Stir in flour and cook, uncovered, on HI (max. power) 1 minute. Stir in broth, wine, salt, and pepper. Cook, covered, on HI (max. power) for 8 minutes. To serve, lightly sprinkle garlic powder on hot buttered toast. Nearly fill microproof soup bowls with hot soup; float toast on top. Cover toast generously with Swiss cheese. Place 2 bowls (or 3, in a circle) in microwave oven. Cook, uncovered, on 70 (roast) 2 minutes, or until cheese is melted.

6 to 8 servings

You may prefer to prepare this soup early in the day. If so, refrigerate before adding toast. Later, cook, covered, on HI (max. power) 5 minutes, stirring twice during heating. Then continue as directed.

3 large onions, thinly
   sliced and quartered
¼ cup butter or margarine
2 teaspoons all-purpose
   flour
6 cups regular-strength beef
   broth
¼ cup dry white wine
½ teaspoon salt
⅛ teaspoon white pepper
   Garlic powder
6 to 8 slices French bread,
   toasted and buttered
1 cup shredded Swiss cheese

Tomato Soup Piquante

Total Cooking Time: 16 to 17 minutes

Place butter and celery in 2-quart glass casserole. Cook on HI (max. power) 5 minutes. Add all other ingredients except lemon slices. Cook, covered, on 80 (reheat) 11 to 12 minutes, or until hot. Let stand 2 to 5 minutes. Garnish with lemon slices.

4 to 6 servings

1 tablespoon butter or
   margarine
½ cup finely chopped celery
1 quart tomato juice
1 can (10½ ounces)
   condensed beef consommé
1 tablespoon dry sherry
½ teaspoon thyme
1 teaspoon sugar
½ teaspoon celery salt
⅛ teaspoon hot-pepper sauce
4 to 6 lemon slices

Cream of Mushroom Soup

Total Cooking Time: 7 minutes

In 2-quart microproof casserole, combine mushrooms, seasonings, and broth. Cook on HI (max. power) 5 minutes, stirring once. Stir in cream, cook on 60 (bake) 2 minutes, or until hot.

6 servings

For a lower-calorie soup, substitute 1 cup evaporated low-fat milk for 1 cup heavy cream.

2 cups chopped fresh
   mushrooms
½ teaspoon onion powder
⅛ teaspoon garlic powder
⅛ teaspoon white pepper
¼ teaspoon salt
2½ cups chicken broth
1 cup heavy cream

Canadian Green Pea Soup

Total Cooking Time: 10½ minutes

1 can (2 ounces) mushroom
    stems and pieces
1 tablespoon butter or
    margarine
2 cans (11½ ounces each)
    condensed green pea
    soup, undiluted
1 cup grated carrots
½ teaspoon salt

In 1-quart measuring cup, drain mushroom liquid, adding enough water to make 2 cups liquid. In 2-quart microproof casserole, melt butter on 60 (bake) 30 seconds. Add mushrooms, soup, and mushroom-water mixture. Stir with fork until well blended. Stir in grated carrots and salt. Cook, covered, on 80 (reheat) 10 minutes, or just until carrots are tender. Serve hot with croutons or crackers.

4 to 6 servings

If you'd like to cut about 100 calories from this recipe, omit the butter.

The temperature probe may be used. Insert into mixture, cook on HI (max. power) at 150°.

Country Vegetable Soup

Total Cooking Time: 40 to 45 minutes

2 medium potatoes, peeled
    and cubed (½ inch)
2 carrots, sliced
2 small onions, chopped
1 cup shredded cabbage
1½ cups fresh corn or 1 can
    (12 ounces) whole-
    kernel corn
4 cups beef stock
1 can (16 ounces) stewed
    tomatoes
1 teaspoon salt
½ teaspoon thyme
⅛ teaspoon pepper
1 bay leaf
⅓ cup chopped fresh parsley

In 4-quart microproof casserole, combine all ingredients except parsley. Cook, covered, on HI (max. power) 20 minutes. Stir, cook on 50 (simmer) 20 to 25 minutes. Let stand 5 minutes. Discard bay leaf. Divide parsley into individual serving dishes. Ladle hot soup over parsley. Serve immediately with crackers or hard rolls.

6 servings

Canadian Green Pea Soup →

New England Clam Chowder
Total Cooking Time: 16 to 19 minutes

2 slices bacon, diced
1 medium onion, chopped
2 medium potatoes, peeled
   and cubed ($\frac{1}{2}$ inch)
$\frac{1}{4}$ cup butter
$\frac{1}{4}$ cup all-purpose flour
2 cans ($7\frac{1}{2}$ ounces each)
   minced clams, drained;
   reserve liquid
3 cups milk
$\frac{1}{2}$ teaspoon salt
$\frac{1}{8}$ teaspoon white pepper

In 3-quart microproof casserole, cook bacon on HI (max. power) 3 minutes. Stir in onion and potatoes. Cook, covered, on 90 (sauté) 8 to 10 minutes, or until potatoes are tender. In 2-cup glass measure melt butter on HI (max. power) 1 minute. Stir in flour, then add to potatoes and onion, mixing well. Add enough water to reserved clam juice to make 2 cups liquid. Stir liquid, clams, milk, salt, and pepper into casserole. Cook, covered, on HI (max. power) 4 to 5 minutes, or until hot. Stir once during cooking.

4 to 6 servings

Mock Lobster Bisque
Total Cooking Time: 22 to 27 minutes

1 package (16 ounces) frozen
   codfish fillets
1 can ($10\frac{3}{4}$ ounces) tomato
   soup
1 can ($10\frac{3}{4}$ ounces) pea
   soup
$\frac{1}{2}$ cup dry sherry
$1\frac{1}{4}$ cups milk

Defrost codfish in package on 30 (defrost) 8 minutes. Separate fillets under cold water. On 9-inch microproof pie plate, place fish fillets with thickest area to outside edge of dish. Cover with well-dampened paper towel. Cook on HI (max. power) 4 minutes. In 3-quart microproof casserole, mix soups, sherry, and milk, stirring until pea soup is dissolved. Flake fish with fork, watching for and discarding any bones. Add fish and drainings, if any, to soup mixture. Cook, covered, on 50 (simmer) 10 to 15 minutes, or until hot but not boiling. Stir once during cooking.

6 servings

Cold Fresh Tomato Soup
Total Cooking Time: 20 to 25 minutes

2 pounds ripe tomatoes,
   peeled, cut in eighths
$\frac{1}{2}$ cup chopped onion
1 2-inch strip lemon
   peel
1 sprig fresh parsley
2 teaspoons paprika
1 tablespoon sugar
1 teaspoon salt
2 cups dry white wine
1 to 2 tablespoons fresh
   lemon juice
$\frac{1}{2}$ cup dairy sour cream or
   yogurt

In 4-quart microproof casserole, combine tomatoes, onion, lemon peel, parsley, paprika, sugar, salt, and wine. Cook, covered, on HI (max. power) 20 to 25 minutes, or until tomatoes are soft and onion cooked. Stir after 10 minutes. Discard lemon peel and parsley sprig. Put tomato mixture in electric blender and purée until smooth. Stir in lemon juice to taste. Chill, covered, for several hours before serving. Top each serving with dollop of sour cream or yogurt.

4 to 6 servings

Minestrone Soup

Total Cooking Time: 43 minutes

Trim meat by removing fat and gristle. Cut into 1/2- to 3/4-inch pieces. In 4-quart microproof casserole, place meat and pour in water. Add onion, pepper, basil, and garlic. Cook, covered, on HI (max. power) 25 minutes, or until meat is tender. Add carrots and tomatoes. Cook, covered, on HI (max. power) 8 minutes. Stir in vermicelli, zucchini, beans, cabbage, parsley, and salt. Cook, covered, on HI (max. power) 10 minutes, stirring once. Allow to stand 5 minutes before serving. Sprinkle generously with cheese.

6 to 8 servings

The temperature probe may be used after all ingredients have been added to casserole. Cook on 60 (bake) set at 150°.

1 pound beef for stew
5 cups hot water
1 medium onion, chopped
1/4 teaspoon pepper
1/2 teaspoon basil
1 clove garlic, minced
1/2 cup thinly sliced carrots
1 can (16 ounces) tomatoes
1/2 cup uncooked vermicelli, broken in 1-inch pieces
1 1/2 cups sliced zucchini
1 can (16 ounces) kidney beans, drained
1 cup shredded cabbage
2 tablespoons chopped fresh parsley
1 teaspoon salt
Grated Parmesan or Romano cheese

Roast Beef 'n Swiss Rolls

Total Cooking Time: 4 1/2 minutes

Mix butter, mustard, onion powder, and poppy seeds in small bowl. Spread butter mixture inside each roll. Top with 1 slice each of beef and cheese. Cover with other half of roll. Wrap each sandwich in paper towel or napkin. Place 2 at a time in oven. Cook on 80 (reheat) 1 1/2 minutes, or until rolls warm.

6 servings

1/4 cup butter or margarine
1 teaspoon prepared mustard
1/2 teaspoon onion powder
1 teaspoon poppy seeds
6 large hard rolls, split
6 thin slices roast beef
6 slices Swiss cheese

Bacon Cheesewiches

Total Cooking Time: 8 to 10 1/2 minutes

Cook bacon according to directions on page 71 until crisp. Drain. Crumble bacon and combine with remaining ingredients except buns. Spread 3 tablespoons bacon-cheese mixture on bottom half of each bun and cover with top. Wrap each sandwich in paper towel. Cook 2 at a time on 80 (reheat) for 1 to 1 1/2 minutes or until heated through.

6 servings

6 slices bacon
1 1/2 cups grated process American cheese
1 tablespoon instant minced onion
1/4 cup catsup
1 tablespoon prepared mustard
6 hamburger buns, split

Sausage and Pepper Heroes

Total Cooking Time: 14 to 16 minutes

Place sausages on microwave roasting rack. Cover with paper towels. Cook on HI (max. power) 4 minutes. Turn sausages. Cook on HI (max. power) 4 minutes longer. Set sausages aside. In a 2-cup glass measure cook barbecue sauce with pepper strips on HI (max. power) 2 minutes. Split hero rolls almost in half. Place 1 cooked sausage in each roll. Top each with one-quarter of the sauce and pepper strips. Place each roll on paper towel-lined microproof plate. Cook, one at a time, on HI (max. power) 1 to 1½ minutes or until rolls are warmed.

4 servings

4   Italian sausages
½   cup Spicy Barbecue Sauce
     (page 158)
1   green pepper, cut in
     strips
4   hero rolls

Bottled barbecue sauce may be substituted for your own.

For party fun, make several batches a day in advance. Combine sausages and barbecue sauce with pepper strips in microproof casserole. Refrigerate. Reheat, using temperature probe inserted in center of casserole. Cook on HI (max. power) set at 150°F.

Hot Dogs in Buns

Total Cooking Time: 2½ to 3 minutes

Place each hot dog in bun and wrap individually in paper towels. Arrange in spoke pattern on glass tray. Cook on 80 (reheat) 2½ to 3 minutes. Watch carefully to avoid overcooking. Serve hot dogs with an assortment of fillings such as chili sauce, prepared mustard, pickle relish, sauerkraut, catsup, chopped onion, chopped green pepper, and grated cheese.

6 servings

6   hot dog buns, split
6   hot dogs

For 1 hot dog only, cook 50 to 60 seconds; 2 hot dogs 1 to 1½ minutes; 3 hot dogs 1½ to 2 minutes; 4 hot dogs 2 to 2¼ minutes.

Hot Ham and Swiss

Total Cooking Time: approximately 1 minute

Spread butter and mayonnaise on bread. Place slices of ham and cheese between bread slices and wrap loosely in paper towel. Insert temperature probe at least 1 inch into the center of sandwich; attach probe to oven receptacle. Cook on HI (max. power) set at 110°F. Let stand 2 minutes before serving.

1 serving

2   slices rye bread
     Butter or margarine
     Mayonnaise
2   thin slices boiled ham
1   slice Swiss cheese

← *Sausage and Pepper Heroes, Hot Dogs in Buns*

Reuben Sandwich
Total Cooking Time: 4 minutes

8 slices dark rye or
    pumpernickel bread, toasted
    Butter or margarine
½ pound thinly sliced
    corned beef
1 can (8 ounces) sauerkraut,
    drained
4 tablespoons Thousand Island
    dressing
4 slices Swiss cheese

Butter toasted bread lightly. Arrange sliced corned beef on 4 slices of toast. Divide sauerkraut among sandwiches. Dot each with 1 tablespoon Thousand Island dressing. Top each with slice of Swiss cheese. Cover with remaining 4 slices of toast, buttered side down. Place each sandwich on a paper plate or paper towel-lined microproof plate. Cook one at a time on 80 (reheat) about 1 minute, or just until cheese is melted.

4 servings

Cheeseburgers
Total Cooking Time: 6 to 10 minutes

1 pound lean ground beef
    Salt and pepper
4 hamburger buns, split and
    toasted
4 slices process American
    cheese

Season ground beef to taste with salt and pepper. Shape into 4 patties. Place in 8-inch round microproof baking dish. Cover with waxed paper, cook on 80 (reheat) 2 minutes. Turn patties over. Cook, covered, on 80 (reheat) 2 to 4 minutes to obtain desired degree of doneness. Place 1 patty on each hamburger bun. Top each patty with a slice of cheese. Place each cheeseburger on a small paper plate. Cook 1 or 2 at a time on 80 (reheat) 1 minute, or until cheese melts. Cover with remaining halves of buns.

4 servings

The microwave browning dish or grill is a popular accessory. It gives hamburgers and other meats their familiar seared, browned appearance. If using your microwave browning dish for cheeseburgers, preheat dish on HI (max. power) for 7 minutes. Put patties in dish and cook on 80 (reheat) for 2 minutes. Repeat for other side of patties. Then proceed with recipe above.

Reuben Sandwich →

Sloppy Joes
Total Cooking Time: 14 minutes

1 pound lean bean ground beef
½ cup chopped onion
½ cup chopped green pepper
½ teaspoon paprika
1 can (6 ounces) tomato
    paste
1 teaspoon salt
    Pinch sugar
    Freshly ground pepper
    to taste
6 hamburger buns, toasted

Crumble beef in 2-quart microproof casserole. Add onion, green pepper, and paprika. Cook, uncovered, on HI (max. power) 4 minutes, or until meat loses its red color, stirring once during cooking time. Break up meat with fork and drain off any fat. Add remaining ingredients except buns; blend well. Cook, covered, on HI (max. power) 10 minutes, stirring twice during cooking time. Spoon onto bottom half of hamburger buns; cover with top half.

6 servings

The Sloppy Joe mixture can be made early in the day and kept in the refrigerator. To serve, remove any congealed fat from top. Spoon desired amount of meat on toasted buns or hard rolls, spreading mixture out to edges. Place single serving on small paper plate. Cook on HI (max. power) 1 to 1½ minutes, until mixture is hot.

Hot Tuna Buns
Total Cooking Time: 2 to 3 minutes

1 can (6½ or 7 ounces)
    tuna, drained
    and flaked
1 cup chopped celery
¼ cup mayonnaise
2 tablespoons catsup
1 teaspoon lemon juice
    Salt and pepper
4 hamburger buns, split

Combine tuna, celery, mayonnaise, catsup, and lemon juice. Season to taste with salt and pepper. Divide tuna mixture among 4 buns. Wrap each sandwich in paper towel or napkin. Cook 2 at a time on 80 (reheat) 1 to 1½ minutes, or until rolls are hot.

4 servings

Chicken and Ham Specials
Total Cooking Time: 9½ to 10½ minutes

4 tablespoons butter or
    margarine
¼ cup all-purpose flour
1 teaspoon salt
⅛ teaspoon pepper
2 cups milk
3 tablespoons dry sherry
2 cups diced cooked chicken
    Paprika
4 English muffins, split and
    buttered
8 thin slices baked ham

Place butter in 4-cup glass measure. Cook on HI (max. power) 1 minute, or until melted. Stir in flour, salt, and pepper. Cook on HI (max. power) 30 seconds. Pour milk in 2-cup glass measure, cook on HI (max. power) 1 minute, or until warm. Briskly stir warm milk into flour mixture until smooth. Cook on HI (max. power) 3 to 4 minutes, stirring twice during cooking. Stir in sherry, chicken, and dash of paprika. Arrange 4 muffin halves on paper towel-lined microproof plate. Place 1 slice ham on each muffin half. Divide half the chicken mixture over ham and sprinkle with paprika. Cook on HI (max. power) 2 minutes, or until heated through. Repeat with remaining 4 muffin halves. Serve hot.

8 servings

Barbecued Beef-on-a-Bun
Total Cooking Time: 19 to 20 minutes

In 2½-quart microproof casserole, cook butter on HI (max. power) 1 minute, or until melted. Cut round steak across grain in very thin strips. Stir into melted butter to coat meat. Cook, covered, on HI (max. power) 4 to 5 minutes, or until meat is no longer pink, stirring twice during cooking.

Dissolve cornstarch in broth and lemon juice. Add to meat. Add all other ingredients, except buns. Stir. Cook, covered, on HI (max. power) 4 minutes. Stir. Cook on 50 (simmer) 10 minutes, stirring once during cooking. Let stand 2 minutes before serving on heated buns.

6 servings

It's hard to imagine a sandwich that is not improved by warming the rolls first. Six rolls heat on 20 (low) 2 to 3 minutes; four rolls take 1 to 1½ minutes.

¼ cup butter or margarine
1 pound top round steak
1½ tablespoons cornstarch
¼ cup beef broth
¼ cup lemon juice
½ cup chili sauce
1 tablespoon brown sugar
½ teaspoon salt
¼ teaspoon paprika
1 tablespoon Worcestershire sauce
1 small clove garlic, minced
1 teaspoon prepared horseradish
1 tablespoon instant minced onion
¼ teaspoon hot-pepper sauce
6 heated buns

Denver Sandwich
Total Cooking Time: 2 minutes

Put all ingredients except bread in 1-cup glass measure; beat with fork. Pour into microproof saucer. Cook on 60 (bake) 1 minute. Stir carefully. Cook on 60 (bake) 1 minute longer, or until set. Serve on toasted bun or bread.

1 sandwich

1 egg
1 tablespoon minced onion
1 teaspoon minced green pepper
3 tablespoons diced boiled ham
Toasted bun or 2 slices toasted bread

Pizza Burgers
Total Cooking Time: 12 to 15 minutes

Crumble ground beef into 1½-quart glass casserole. Add onion and cover with casserole lid. Cook on HI (max. power) 4 minutes. Stir to break up meat into small pieces. Continue to cook on HI (max. power) 1 to 2 minutes more. Drain off juices. Stir in salt, pepper, cinnamon, and pizza sauce. Cook, covered, on HI (max. power) 5 to 6 minutes, or until hot and bubbly. Stir in ½ cup mozzarella. Arrange 4 bottom halves of buns on microproof plate. Spoon on half the meat mixture. Sprinkle each with 1 tablespoon cheese. Top with other half of buns. Cook on HI (max. power) 1 to 1½ minutes, or until cheese just starts to melt. Repeat for remaining buns. Serve hot.

8 servings

1 pound lean ground beef
2 tablespoons finely chopped onion
½ teaspoon salt
⅛ teaspoon pepper
¼ teaspoon cinnamon
¾ cup pizza sauce
1 cup shredded mozzarella cheese
8 hamburger buns, split

Hot Cranberry Punch

Total Cooking Time: 9 to 11 minutes

In 2-quart microproof casserole combine juices, spices, and sugar. Cook, covered, on HI (max. power) 9 to 11 minutes, or until mixture comes to a boil. Strain into warmed punch bowl. Garnish with clove-studded orange slices.

8 servings

1	cup apple juice
3	cups cranberry juice
½	cup orange juice
3	tablespoons lemon juice
4	whole cloves
1	cinnamon stick
3	tablespoons sugar
1	orange, sliced
	Whole cloves

Hot Buttered Rum

Total Cooking Time: 1½ to 2 minutes

In tall microproof mug or cup, mix brown sugar and rum. Add water to two-thirds full. Cook on HI (max. power) 1½ to 2 minutes, until very hot but not boiling. Add butter; sprinkle with nutmeg. Add cinnamon stick.

1 serving

2	teaspoons brown sugar
¼	cup light or dark rum
1½	teaspoons sweet butter
	Dash nutmeg
	Cinnamon stick

Russian Tea Mix

Total Cooking Time: 1½ to 2 minutes

Mix all ingredients and store in covered jar or container until ready to use. For 1 serving, place 1 or 2 teaspoons mix in microproof cup. Add water or cider, cook on HI (max. power) 1½ to 2 minutes.

64 servings

1	jar (9 ounces) powdered orange breakfast drink
1	package (3 ounces) lemonade mix
⅓	cup sugar
1½	cups instant unsweetened tea
1	teaspoon cinnamon
¾	teaspoon ground ginger
1	teaspoon ground cloves
¼	teaspoon nutmeg
	Water or apple cider

For a lower-calorie drink, substitute artificial sweetener to equal ⅓ cup sugar. If you'd like to serve your guests the regular mix but fix a low-calorie one for yourself, place ½ teaspoon grated orange peel, 1 whole clove, 1½ teaspoons instant unsweetened tea, and 1 cup water in microproof mug. Heat on HI (max. power) 1½ minutes. Add artificial sweetener equal to 2 teaspoons sugar or to taste and stir with cinnamon stick.

← *Hot Cranberry Punch, Hot Buttered Rum, West Coast Cocoa (page 64), Hot Devilish Daiquiri (page 64), Russian Tea*

Irish Coffee

Total Cooking Time: 1½ to 2 minutes

3 tablespoons Irish whiskey
2 teaspoons sugar
1 tablespoon instant coffee
  Whipped cream

Measure whiskey into 8-ounce microproof glass or mug. Add sugar and coffee. Add water until container is three-fourths full, mix well. Cook on HI (max. power) 1½ to 2 minutes until hot, but not boiling. Stir to dissolve sugar. Top with dollop of whipped cream. Do not stir. Coffee should be sipped through the layer of cream.

1 serving

Hot Devilish Daiquiri

Total Cooking Time: 5½ to 6½ minutes

1½ cups hot water
¼ cup sugar
2 sticks cinnamon
8 whole cloves
1 can (6 ounces) frozen
    lemonade concentrate
1 can (6 ounces) frozen
    limeade concentrate
½ cup light rum

In a 2-quart microproof casserole, combine hot water, sugar, spices, and concentrated fruit juices. Stir, then cook on HI (max. power) 5 to 6 minutes, or until mixture boils. Heat rum in a microproof container on HI (max. power) for 30 seconds. Ignite and pour over hot beverage. Ladle into punch cups for serving.

8 to 10 servings

West Coast Cocoa

Total Cooking Time: 6 to 7 minutes

⅓ cup cocoa
¼ cup sugar
3 cups milk
2 teaspoons grated orange
    rind
¼ teaspoon almond extract
4 cinnamon sticks

Combine cocoa and sugar in 4-cup glass measure. Add ½ cup milk to make smooth paste. Stir in remaining milk, orange rind, and almond extract. Blend thoroughly to dissolve sugar. Cook on 70 (roast) 6 to 7 minutes, or until hot. Pour into mugs and place cinnamon sticks in drinks, as stirrers.

4 servings

Tomato Warmer

Total Cooking Time: 6 to 7 minutes

2½ cups tomato juice
1 can (10½ ounces)
    condensed beef broth
¼ cup lemon juice
1 teaspoon prepared
    horseradish
1 teaspoon parsley flakes
½ teaspoon celery salt
4 tablespoons dry sherry
    (optional)

In a 4-cup microproof container, combine all ingredients except sherry. Cook on HI (max. power) 6 to 7 minutes, until hot but not boiling. Pour into 6 mugs and stir 2 teaspoons sherry into each mug.

6 servings

RING THE DINNER BELL FOR MEAT

Cooking meat in the microwave oven offers tremendous advantages over the conventional range. For juiciness and flavor, the microwave method excels. It also stretches your meat dollar by reducing shrinkage. And you can defrost, cook, and reheat in minutes while your kitchen remains cool and comfortable.

If some of your guests or family prefer beef rare and others well done, the microwave oven solves the problem. After the roast is carved, a few seconds in the microwave oven will bring slices of rare roast to medium or well done. In addition, meat for the barbecue is enhanced by precooking in the microwave. You get that wonderful charcoal flavor without the long watchful cooking that often results in burned or blackened meat. Microwave roasting methods are similar to dry roasting in your conventional oven. This means that the better, tender cuts of meat are recommended for best results. Less tender cuts should be marinated or tenderized and cooked at low power settings. As in conventional cooking, they are braised or stewed to achieve tenderness.

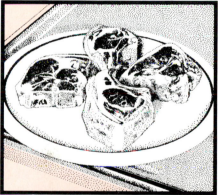

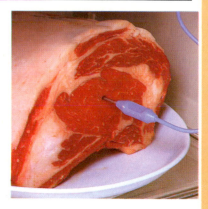

Meatloaf may be cooked in a loaf, but a ring mold is best. You can make your own ring mold by using a small straight-sided glass in baking dish (above). Food arrangement for microwave cooking is illustrated with lamb chops: the narrow bony end is placed toward the center of the dish (above right). Placement of the temperature probe in a rib roast (right).

Some people believe that meat does not brown in microwave ovens. Wrong! Any meat that cooks more than 10 minutes will brown in your microwave oven. True, individual steaks, chops, ground meat patties, and thin cuts of meat that cook quickly will brown best with a microproof browning dish.

Using the browning dish for Cheeseburgers (page 58). →

Converting Your Recipes

Charts on the following pages outline microwave thawing and cooking times for the standard cuts of meat. The temperature probe eliminates any guesswork or troublesome arithmetic. For converting casseroles, meatloaf, meat in sauces, and recipes that call for less tender cuts of meat, you're sure to find a similar recipe here to guide your own creations. Adapt your conventional recipes by matching ingredients and methods as closely as possible. Experiment as much as you like. Here are some helpful hints:

- ☐ For best results, cook evenly shaped, boned, rolled, and tied small roasts.
- ☐ Recipe times here presume meat is at refrigerator temperature. If your meal requires lengthy preparation, during which the meat may reach room temperature, reduce cooking times.
- ☐ Baste, marinate, or season meat just as you would for conventional cooking. However, avoid salting the surface before or during cooking, since salt tends to draw liquids from foods.
- ☐ You can use a microwave roasting rack to elevate meat from its drippings during cooking.
- ☐ Use a tight cover and a 40 (braise) or 50 (simmer) setting for the less tender cuts of meat such as chuck, bottom round, brisket, and stewing meat cooked in liquid.
- ☐ Check dishes that use relatively long cooking times to be sure liquid has not evaporated. Add liquid as necessary.
- ☐ Enhance the color and flavor of ground beef patties, steaks, meatloaf, and roasts by using one of the following: powdered brown gravy mix; a liquid browning agent; Worcestershire, soy sauce or steak sauce; paprika; cooked bacon; tomato sauce; or dehydrated onion soup mix.
- ☐ Most ground beef recipes call for lean meat. If you are using regular ground beef, drain fat before adding sauce ingredients.
- ☐ Large cuts not usually cooked on the charcoal grill, such as ham, leg of lamb, pork roast, turkey, and whole chicken, may be partially cooked in the microwave oven and finished on the grill for a lovely charcoal flavor and a browned crispness. It's also a great time saver for spareribs.

Using the Defrosting Guide

1. You may defrost meat within its original paper or plastic wrappings. Remove all metal rings, wire twist ties, and all foil wrapping.
2. Place meat in microproof dish.
3. Defrost in the microwave oven only as long as necessary, since standing time will complete the thawing process. Separate items like chops, bacon slices, and frankfurters into pieces as soon as possible. If separated pieces are not thawed, distribute them evenly in oven and continue defrosting.
4. Slightly increase the time for weights larger than on the chart. Do not double.
5. If you do not plan immediate cooking, follow the guide for only one-half to three-fourths of recommended time. Place meat in refrigerator to continue defrosting until needed.

DEFROSTING GUIDE — MEAT

Meat	Amount	Cook Control Setting	Time (in minutes per pound)	Standing Time (in minutes)	Special Notes
Ground beef	1-lb.	30 (defrost)	5 - 6	5	Turn over once. Remove thawed portions with fork. Return remainder. Freeze in doughnut shape. Depress center when freezing. Defrost on plate.
	2-lbs.	30 (defrost)	8 - 9	5	
	1/4-lb. patty	30 (defrost)	1 per patty	2	
Pot roast, chuck	under 4 lbs.	30 (defrost)	3 - 5	10	Turn over once.
	over 4 lbs.	70 (roast)	3 - 5	10	Turn over once.
Rib roast, rolled	3 to 4 lbs.	30 (defrost)	6 - 8	30 - 45	Turn over once.
	6 to 8 lbs.	70 (roast)	6 - 8	90	Turn over twice.
Rib roast, bone in		70 (roast)	5 - 6	45 - 90	Turn over twice.
Rump roast	3 to 4 lbs.	30 (defrost)	3 - 5	30	Turn over once.
	6 to 7 lbs.	70 (roast)	3 - 5	45	Turn over twice.
Round steak		30 (defrost)	4 - 5	5 - 10	Turn over once.
Flank steak		30 (defrost)	4 - 5	5 - 10	Turn over once.
Sirloin steak	1/2" thick	30 (defrost)	4 - 5	5 - 10	Turn over once.
Tenderloin		30 (defrost)	5 - 6	10	Turn over once.
Steaks	2 or 3 2 to 3 lbs.	30 (defrost)	4 - 5	8 - 10	Turn over once.
Stew beef	2 lbs.	30 (defrost)	3 - 5	8 - 10	Turn over once. Separate.
Lamb					
Cubed for stew		30 (defrost)	7 - 8	5	Turn over once. Separate.
Ground lamb	under 4 lbs.	30 (defrost)	3 - 5	30 - 45	Turn over once.
	over 4 lbs.	70 (roast)	3 - 5	30 - 45	Turn over twice.
Chops	1" thick	30 (defrost)	5 - 8	15	Turn over twice.
Leg	5 - 8 lbs.	30 (defrost)	4 - 5	15 - 20	Turn over twice.
Pork					
Chops	1/2"	30 (defrost)	4 - 6	5 - 10	Separate chops halfway through defrosting time.
	1"	30 (defrost)	5 - 7	10	
Spareribs, country-style ribs		30 (defrost)	5 - 7	10	Turn over once.
Roast	under 4 lbs.	30 (defrost)	4 - 5	30 - 45	Turn over once.
	over 4 lbs.	70 (roast)	4 - 5	30 - 45	Turn over twice.
Bacon	1-lb.	30 (defrost)	2 - 3	3 - 5	Defrost until strips separate.
Sausage, bulk	1 lb.	30 (defrost)	2 - 3	3 - 5	Turn over once. Remove thawed portions with fork. Return remainder.
Sausage links	1 lb.	30 (defrost)	3 - 5	4 - 6	Turn over once. Defrost until pieces can be separated.
Hot dogs		30 (defrost)	5 - 6	5	

DEFROSTING GUIDE — MEAT

Meat	Amount	Cook Control Setting	Time (in minutes) per pound)	Standing Time (in minutes)	Special Notes
Veal					
Roast	3 to 4 lbs.	30 (defrost)	5 - 7	30	Turn over once.
	6 to 7 lbs.	70 (roast)	5 - 7	90	Turn over twice.
Chops	1/2″ thick	30 (defrost)	4 - 6	20	Turn over once. Separate chops and continue defrosting.
Variety Meat					
Liver		30 (defrost)	5 - 6	10	Turn over once.
Tongue		30 (defrost)	7 - 8	10	Turn over once.

Using the Cooking Guide

1. Meat should be completely thawed before cooking.
2. Place meat fat side down, on microwave roasting rack set in glass baking dish.
3. Meat may be covered lightly with waxed paper to stop splatters.
4. Use the temperature probe for the most accurate cooking of larger meats. Place probe sensor as horizontally as possible in the densest area, avoiding fat pockets or bone.
5. Unless otherwise noted, times given for steaks and patties will give medium doneness.
6. Ground meat to be used for casseroles should be cooked briefly first; crumble it into a microproof dish and cook covered with a paper towel. Then drain off any fat and add meat to casserole.
7. During standing time, the internal temperature of roasts will rise approximately 15°. Hence, standing time is considered an essential part of the time required to complete cooking.
8. Cutlets and chops that are breaded are cooked at the same time and cook control setting as shown on chart.

COOKING GUIDE — MEAT

Meat	Amount	First Cook Control Setting And Time	Second Cook Control Setting And Time	or	Temperature Probe And Cook Control Setting	Standing Time (in minutes)	Special Notes
Beef							
Ground beef	Bulk	HI (max. power) 2½ minutes per pound	Stir. HI (max. power) 2½ minutes per pound			5	Crumble in dish, cook covered.
Ground beef patties, 4 oz., 1/2″ thick	1	HI (max. power) 1 minute	Turn over. HI (max. power) 1 - 1½ minutes				Shallow baking dish.
	2	HI (max. power) 1 - 1½ minutes	Turn over. HI (max. power) 1 - 1½ minutes				Shallow baking dish.
	4	HI (max. power) 3 minutes	Turn over. HI (max. power) 3 - 3½ minutes				Shallow baking dish.
Meatloaf	2 lbs.	HI (max. power) 12 - 14 minutes		or	HI (max. power) 160°	5 - 10	Glass loaf dish or glass ring mold.

COOKING GUIDE — MEAT

Meat	Amount	First Cook Control Setting And Time	Second Cook Control Setting And Time	or	Temperature Probe And Cook Control Setting	Standing Time (in minutes)	Special Notes
Beef rib roast, boneless		HI (max. power) Rare: 4-5 minutes per pound Medium: 5-6 minutes per pound Well: 6-7 minutes per pound	Turn over. 70 (roast) 3-4 minutes per pound 5-6 minutes per pound 6-7 minutes per pound	or	Turn over once. 70 (roast) 120° 130° 140°	10 10 10	Glass baking dish with microproof roasting rack.
Rib roast, bone in		HI (max. power) Rare: 3-4 minutes per pound Medium: 4-5 minutes per pound Well: 5-6 minutes per pound	Turn over. 70 (roast) 3-4 minutes per pound 3-5 minutes per pound 5-6 minutes per pound	or	Turn over once. 70 (roast) 120° 130° 140°	10	Glass baking dish with microproof roasting rack.
Beef round, rump, or chuck, boneless		HI (max. power) 5 minutes per pound	Turn over. 50 (simmer) 10 minutes per pound			10-15	Casserole with tight cover. Requires liquid.
Beef brisket, boneless, fresh or corned	2½-3½ lbs.	HI (max. power) 5 minutes per pound	Turn over. 50 (simmer) 20 minutes per pound			10-15	4-quart casserole Dutch oven with tight cover. Water to cover.
Top round steak		HI (max. power) 5 minutes per pound	Turn over. 50 (simmer) 5 minutes per pound			10-15	Casserole with tight cover. Requires liquid.
Sirloin steak	3/4 to 1" thick	HI (max. power) 4½ minutes per pound	Drain dish and turn over. HI (max. power) 2 minutes per pound			10-15	Shallow cooking dish or browning dish preheated 8 minutes on HI (max. power).
Minute steak or cube steak,	4, 6-oz. steaks	HI (max. power) 1-2 minutes	Drain dish and turn over. HI (max. power) 1-2 minutes				Browning dish preheated on HI (max. power) 8 minutes.
Tenderloin	4, 8-oz. steaks	HI (max. power) Rare: 5 minutes Med: 6 minutes Well: 9 minutes	Drain, turn steak. HI (max. power) 1-2 minutes 2-3 minutes 2-3 minutes			10-15	Browning dish preheated on HI (max. power) 8 minutes.
Rib eye or strip steak	1½ to 2 lbs.	HI (max. power) Rare: 4 minutes Med: 5 minutes Well: 7 minutes	Drain, turn steak. HI (max. power) ½-1 minute 1-2 minutes 2-3 minutes			10-15	Browning dish preheated on HI (max. power) 8 minutes.
Lamb Ground lamb patties	1-2 lbs.	HI (max. power) 4 minutes	Turn over. HI (max. power) 4-5 minutes				Browning dish preheated on HI (max. power) 7 minutes.
Lamb chops	1-1½ lbs. 1" thick	HI (max. power) 8 minutes	Turn over. HI (max. power) 7-8 minutes				Browning dish preheated on HI (max. power) 7 minutes.
Lamb leg or shoulder roast, bone in		70 (roast) Medium: 4-5 minutes per pound Well: 5-6 minutes per pound	Cover end of leg bone with foil. Turn over. 70 (roast) Medium: 4-5 minutes per pound Well: 5-6 minutes per pound	or	Turn over once. Cover end of leg bone with foil. 145° 165°	5 10	12×7-inch dish with microproof roasting rack.

COOKING GUIDE — MEAT

Meat	Amount	First Cook Control Setting And Time	Second Cook Control Setting And Time	or	Temperature Probe And Cook Control Setting	Standing Time (in minutes)	Special Notes
Lamb roast, boneless		70 (roast) 5 - 6 minutes per pound	Turn over. 70 (roast) 5 - 6 minutes per pound	or	Turn over once. 70 (roast) 150°	10	12 × 7-inch dish with microproof roasting rack.
Veal: Shoulder or rump roast, boneless	2 - 5 lbs.	70 (roast) 9 minutes per pound	Turn over. 70 (roast) 9 - 10 minutes per pound	or	Turn over once. 70 (roast) 155°	10	12 × 7-inch dish with microproof roasting rack.
Veal cutlets or loin chops	1/2" thick	HI (max. power) 2 minutes per pound	Turn over. HI (max. power) 2 - 3½ minutes per pound				Browning dish preheated on HI (max. power) 7 - 10 minutes.
Pork: Pork chops	1/2" thick	HI (max. power) 6 minutes per pound	Turn over. HI (max. power) 5 - 6 minutes per pound			5	Browning dish preheated on HI (max. power) 7 minutes
Spareribs		70 (roast) 6 - 7 minutes per pound	Turn over. 70 (roast) 6 - 7 minutes per pound			10	12 × 7-inch dish with microproof roasting rack.
Pork loin roast, boneless	3 - 5 lbs.	HI (max. power) 6 minutes per pound	Turn over. 70 (roast) 5 - 6 minutes per pound	or	Turn over once. 70 (roast) 165°	10	12 × 7-inch dish with microproof roasting rack.
Pork loin, center cut	4 - 5 lbs.	HI (max. power) 5 - 6 minutes per pound	Turn over. 4 - 5 minutes per pound 70 (roast)	or	Turn over once. 70 (roast) 165°	10	13 × 9-inch dish with microproof roasting rack.
Ham, boneless, precooked		70 (roast) 5 - 7 minutes per pound	Turn over. 70 (roast) 5 - 7 minutes per pound	or	Turn over once. 120° 70 (roast)	10	12 × 7-inch dish with microproof roasting rack.
Center cut ham slice	1 - 1½ lbs.	70 (roast) 5 minutes per pound	Turn over. 70 (roast) 5 - 6 minutes per pound	or	Turn over once. 120° 70 (roast)	10	12 × 7-inch baking dish.
Smoked ham shank		70 (roast) 4 - 5 minutes per pound	Turn over. 70 (roast) 4 - 5 minutes per pound	or	Turn over once. 120° 70 (roast)	10	12 × 7-inch dish with microproof roasting rack.
Canned ham	3 lbs.	70 (roast) 5 - 6 minutes per pound	70 (roast) 5 - 6 minutes per pound	or or	120° 70 (roast)	10	12 × 7-inch dish with microproof roasting rack.
	5 lbs.	70 (roast) 4 - 5 minutes per pound	Turn over. 70 (roast) 4 - 5 minutes per pound	or	Turn over once. 120° 70 (roast)	10	12 × 7-inch dish with microproof roasting rack.
Sausage patties	12-oz.	HI (max. power) 2 minutes	Turn over. HI (max. power) 1½ - 2 minutes per pound				Browning dish preheated on HI (max. power) 7 minutes.
Sausage	16 oz.	HI (max. power) 3 minutes	Stir. HI (max. power) 1 - 2 minutes				Crumble into 1½-quart dish, covered.
Pork sausage links	1/2 lb.	Pierce casing HI (max. power) 1 minute	Turn over. HI (max. power) 1 - 1½ minutes				Browning dish preheated on HI (max. power) 7 minutes.
	1 lb.	HI (max. power) 2 minutes	HI (max. power) 1½ - 2 minutes				

COOKING GUIDE — MEAT

Meat	Amount	First Cook Control Setting And Time	Second Cook Control Setting And Time	or	Temperature Probe And Cook Control Setting	Standing Time (in minutes)	Special Notes
Bratwurst, precooked		Pierce casing 70 (roast) 5 minutes per pound	Rearrange. 70 (roast) 4-5 minutes per pound				Casserole.
Polish sausage, knockwurst, ring bologna		Pierce casing 80 (reheat) 2-2½ minutes per pound	Rearrange 80 (reheat) 2-2½ minutes per pound				Casserole.
Hot dogs	1	80 (reheat) 25-30 seconds					Shallow dish.
	2	80 (reheat) 25-40 seconds					Shallow dish.
	4	80 (reheat) 50-55 seconds					Shallow dish.
Bacon 2 slices		HI (max. power) 2-2½ minutes					Dish; slices between paper towels
4 slices		HI (max. power) 4-4½ minutes					Dish; slices between paper towels
6 slices		HI (max. power) 5-6 minutes					Roasting rack, slices covered with paper towels
8 slices		HI (max. power) 6-7 minutes					Roasting rack, slices covered with paper towels

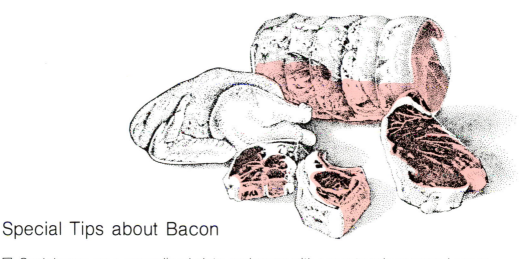

Special Tips about Bacon

☐ Cook bacon on a paper-lined plate, and cover with paper towels or waxed paper to prevent splatters and absorb drippings.

☐ To reserve drippings, cook bacon on a meat rack in a baking dish or on a microwave bacon rack. Bacon can also be cooked, in slices or cut up, in a casserole and removed if necessary with a slotted spoon.

☐ For bacon that is soft rather than crisp, cook at the minimum timing.

☐ Bacon varies in quality. The thickness and amount of sugar and salt used in curing will affect browning and timing. Cook thicker slices a bit longer than the chart indicates. You will also find that sweeter bacon cooks more quickly.

☐ Sugar in bacon causes brown spots to appear on the paper towels. If the bacon tends to stick a bit to the towel, it is due to an extra high amount of sugar.

COOKING/DEFROSTING GUIDE — CONVENIENCE BEEF

Food	Amount	Cook Control Setting	Time (in minutes)	or	Temperature Probe Setting	Special Notes
Barbecued beef, chili, stew, hash, meatballs, etc.	16 oz. or less (cans)	80 (reheat)	3 - 5	or	150°	Remove from cans to microproof plate or casserole, cover. Stir halfway through cooking time.
Stuffed peppers, cabbage rolls, chow mein, etc.	16 - 32 oz. (cans)	80 (reheat)	5 - 9	or	150°	
Barbecued beef, chili, stew, corned beef hash, meatballs, patties in sauce, gravy	8 - 16 oz. package (frozen)	HI (max. power)	5 - 11	or	150°	Remove from foil container to microproof casserole, cover. Slit plastic pouches
Dry casserole mixes, cooked hamburger added	6½ - 8 oz. package	HI (max. power)	18 - 22	or	150°	Remove mix from package to 3-quart microproof casserole. Cover. Stir once.

Meatballs à la Russe
Total Cooking Time: 16 minutes

1½   pounds lean ground beef
½   cup milk
1   package (1¼ ounces) onion soup mix, divided
3   tablespoons all-purpose flour
1½   cups water
2   tablespoons chopped fresh parsley
½   cup dairy sour cream

In large bowl, combine beef with milk and 2 tablespoons of soup mix. Mix thoroughly. Shape into 24 small meatballs. Place in 3-quart oval microproof baking dish. Cover with waxed paper and cook on HI (max. power) 3 minutes. Turn meatballs over. Cook, covered, on HI (max. power) 2 minutes. Remove meatballs. Stir flour into drippings. Stir in water, parsley and remaining soup mix. Cook, uncovered, on 60 (bake) 5 minutes, or until mixture comes to a boil. Add meatballs. Cook, covered, on 60 (bake) 6 minutes, stirring occasionally. Gradually blend in sour cream. Let stand, covered, 5 minutes before serving. Serve over hot cooked rice or noodles.

6 servings

Boiled Beef Carbonnade
Total Cooking Time: 1 hour 40 minutes to 1 hour 45 minutes

2½   to 3 pounds lean beef heel of round roast
1   onion, sliced
1   carrot, sliced
5   peppercorns
1   bay leaf
1   can beer (12 ounces)
⅛   teaspoon white pepper
Salt to taste

Place all ingredients except salt in 4-quart microproof bowl, add water to cover. Cook, covered, on HI (max. power) 30 minutes. Turn meat, add more water if necessary. Cook, covered, on 50 (simmer) 60 minutes. Let stand 10 minutes. If not fork tender, return to oven and cook, covered, on 50 (simmer) 10 to 15 minutes. Remove meat and set aside. Strain broth and skim off fat. Slice meat thinly, and serve with broth. Season to taste.

6 servings

Oriental Beef

Total Cooking Time: 10 to 12 minutes

In 2-quart oval microproof baking dish, combine soy sauce, sherry, water, sugar, garlic, and ginger. Add steak strips and stir. Cover with plastic wrap and let stand at room temperature 4 hours, stirring occasionally. Cut onions into 2-inch pieces, including green part. Cut broccoli stems diagonally into thin slices; break flowerets into individual pieces. Rinse bean sprouts in cold water and drain. Push meat to center of dish. Place onions, broccoli, bean sprouts and water chestnuts in mixed arrangement around meat. Cover dish with plastic wrap. Cook on HI (max. power) 10 to 12 minutes. Remove from oven and let stand 2 minutes. Serve with hot cooked rice.

4 to 6 servings

½ cup soy sauce
½ cup dry sherry
½ cup water
1 tablespoon sugar
1 clove garlic, minced
2 thin slices fresh ginger, minced
1½ to 2 pounds boneless sirloin steak, cut into thin strips
6 green onions
½ bunch fresh broccoli or 1 package (10 ounces) frozen broccoli spears, thawed
½ pound fresh bean sprouts or 2 cups canned bean sprouts, drained
1 can (5 ounces) water chestnuts, drained and sliced

Short Ribs of Beef

Total Cooking Time: 45 minutes

Arrange short ribs in 3-quart microproof casserole. Sprinkle with garlic and salt. Combine wine and browning sauce. Pour over short ribs. Cover with plastic wrap and cook on 50 (simmer) 45 minutes, or until meat is tender. Remove and let stand 5 minutes.

4 servings

2 pounds meaty short ribs of beef
1 clove garlic, minced
½ teaspoon salt
½ cup dry red wine
1 tablespoon browning sauce

Beef Roulade

Total Cooking Time: 49 minutes

Pound steak with meat mallet or edge of saucer. Cut into 6 3-inch wide pieces. In 1-quart glass measure, combine butter, celery, and onion. Cook on HI (max. power) 4 minutes, or until onion is transparent. Stir in bread crumbs, rosemary, thyme, and pepper. Spread stuffing on top of steak. Roll meat around stuffing and fasten with toothpicks. Arrange in 2-quart microproof baking dish. Spoon soup over top of meat rolls. Cook on 50 (simmer) for 45 minutes, or until meat is tender. Turn meat once during cooking time, spooning mushroom soup over top of meat rolls. Let stand 5 minutes before serving.

6 servings

2 pounds top round steak, ½-inch thick
2 tablespoons butter or margarine
½ cup chopped celery with leaves
¼ cup chopped onion
1 cup soft bread crumbs
¼ teaspoon rosemary
¼ teaspoon thyme
¼ teaspoon pepper
1 can (10¾ ounces) condensed cream of mushroom soup, undiluted

Tenderloin of Beef Supreme
Total Cooking Time: 15 minutes

2 to 2½ pounds beef
   tenderloin roast
3 tablespoons dehydrated
   onion soup mix
½ pound mushrooms, sliced

In shallow dish, place roast and pat meat evenly with soup mix. Arrange mushrooms on top of roast. Cook, covered, with waxed paper, on HI (max. power) 5 minutes. Turn roast over and spoon mushrooms and drippings over top. Cook, covered, on HI (max. power) 5 minutes. Continue cooking on 70 (roast) 5 minutes for medium rare. Let stand 5 to 10 minutes before serving.

4 servings

If using temperature probe, insert horizontally set at 125° for medium rare.

Hungarian Goulash
Total Cooking Time: 55 to 60 minutes

4 large tomatoes
2 pounds beef for stew, cut
   in 1-inch cubes
1 onion, coarsely chopped
1 teaspoon salt
½ teaspoon freshly ground
   pepper
1½ tablespoons paprika
1 cup dairy sour cream

Peel and seed tomatoes, cut in chunks. Place beef, onion, salt, pepper, and paprika in 3-quart microproof casserole. Add tomatoes, stir. Cook, covered, on 70 (roast) 55 to 60 minutes, or until beef is tender, stirring twice during cooking. Stir sour cream gradually into mixture and let stand, covered, 5 minutes.

4 to 6 servings

Pepper Steak
Total Cooking Time: 24 to 27 minutes

1 to 1½ pounds top round
   steak, ½ inch thick
1 tablespoon vegetable oil
1 clove garlic, minced
2 teaspoons cornstarch
2 tablespoons soy sauce
½ cup water
1 teaspoon instant beef
   bouillon
2 cups 1-inch chunks green
   pepper
1 cup thinly sliced onion
2 large stalks celery,
   sliced
1 jar (2-ounces) pimiento,
   chopped
1 teaspoon salt
¼ teaspoon pepper

Cut steak in thin strips. Preheat browning dish on HI (max. power) 7 minutes. Smear oil over dish and add beef strips. Cook on HI (max. power) 2 to 3 minutes, flipping strips after 1 minute, or when strips are brown. Stir; add garlic. Cook, covered, on 70 (roast) 7 minutes. Dissolve cornstarch in soy sauce and add to meat. If your browning dish is too small to hold meat and remaining ingredients transfer to 2-quart casserole. Stir. Blend in remaining ingredients. Cook, covered, on HI (max. power) 8 to 10 minutes, or until vegetables are just tender. Let stand 5 minutes before serving.

4 servings

Beef and Peppers

Total Cooking Time: 8 to 9 minutes

Pour oil in 3-quart microproof casserole or baking dish. Add beef strips and stir to coat with oil. Add onion, garlic, salt, pepper, and tomatoes. Cover and cook on HI (max. power) 4 minutes, stirring once during cooking. Add green peppers and soy sauce, stir. Cook, covered, on HI (max. power) 4 to 5 minutes, or until green pepper is just tender. Serve with hot cooked rice or chow mein noodles.

4 servings

2 tablespoons vegetable oil
1 pound top round or sirloin
   steak, cut into thin strips
1 medium onion, finely chopped
1 clove garlic, minced
1 teaspoon salt
⅛ teaspoon pepper
1 can (16 ounces) tomatoes,
   broken up
2 large green peppers, cut
   in strips
2 tablespoons soy sauce

Pot Roast in Sherry

Total Cooking Time: 45 to 50 minutes

Trim all fat from roast. Place in a 12 × 7-inch glass baking dish. Sprinkle with onion soup mix. Pour sherry and broth over roast. Cover dish tightly with plastic wrap. Cook on 70 (roast) 10 minutes. Reduce power to 50 (simmer) and cook 15 minutes. Turn roast over and baste with juices. Cover tightly again. Cook on 50 (simmer) 20 to 25 minutes, or until meat is tender. Let stand 10 minutes. Use drippings for gravy (see page 153).

6 to 8 servings

1 3-pound lean beef chuck
   roast
1 envelope dry onion soup
   mix
½ cup dry sherry
½ cup beef broth

Shish Kabob

Total Cooking Time: 2 to 4½ minutes

Make marinade by combining vinegar, oil, onion salt, garlic, soy sauce, oregano, and water in large mixing bowl. Cut meat into 1-inch cubes. Add to marinade and let stand refrigerated 5 to 6 hours, stirring occasionally. Arrange meat cubes and vegetables alternately on 6 long wooden skewers. Place 2 or 3 skewers at a time on microproof dinner plate. Cook, uncovered, on HI (max. power) 1 to 1½ minutes for medium rare. Repeat for remaining skewers. Cook slightly longer for well done meat.

6 servings

The time and ingredients in this recipe may be cut in half for three servings. Marinating time stays the same. (Can't find wooden skewers? Use chopsticks!)

½ cup wine vinegar
½ cup vegetable oil
1 teaspoon onion salt
1 clove garlic, cut in half
¼ cup soy sauce
1 teaspoon oregano
½ cup water
2 pounds boneless sirloin
   steak or boneless
   lamb shoulder roast
½ pound small mushrooms
12 tomato wedges or cherry
   tomatoes (very firm)
1 green pepper, cut in
   1-inch squares

Irish Stew

Total Cooking Time: 1 hour 30 minutes to 1 hour 40 minutes

2 pounds beef for stew, cut
   in 1-inch cubes
½ teaspoon salt
1 package (1½ ounces)
   brown gravy mix with
   mushrooms
1 cup water
3 stalks celery, cut in
   1-inch slices
3 medium carrots, sliced
3 medium potatoes, peeled
   and cut in eighths

Place beef cubes in 3-quart microproof casserole or baking dish. Sprinkle with salt. Stir together gravy mix and water. Pour over meat. Cook, covered, on 70 (roast) 50 minutes, stirring once during cooking. Add vegetables and mix to cover with gravy. Cook, covered, on 50 (simmer) 40 to 50 minutes, or until vegetables and meat are tender. Let stand 5 minutes before serving.

4 to 6 servings

Irish Stew freezes very well; you might like to serve half and freeze the remainder. If you prefer to cut the recipe in half, you may halve the ingredients but cook 40 minutes on 70 (roast). After adding vegetables, cook on 50 (simmer) 30 to 35 minutes, or until tender.

Thaw a whole Irish Stew on 30 (defrost) 10 minutes, or until stew can be removed from container. Carefully stir during thawing to even the heat distribution. Finish heating on 70 (roast) about 20 minutes. For half the recipe, thaw, as above, 6 or 7 minutes, and reheat 10 to 12 minutes.

Stuffed Cabbage

Total Cooking Time: 36 minutes

1 head cabbage, about 1½
   pounds
¼ cup water
1 pound lean ground beef
½ pound ground pork
¾ cup cooked rice
1 egg, lightly beaten
½ teaspoon thyme
1 tablespoon chopped fresh
   parsley
1 clove garlic, minced
1 teaspoon salt
¼ teaspoon pepper
¼ cup butter or margarine
1 can (16 ounces) tomato
   sauce

Remove core and blemished leaves of cabbage. Place cabbage in 3-quart microproof casserole. Add water. Cover with plastic wrap and cook on HI (max. power) 6 minutes. Cool cabbage slightly and separate leaves. Combine ground beef, pork, rice, egg, thyme, parsley, garlic, salt, and pepper; stir thoroughly. Divide mixture among 6 to 8 large cabbage leaves. Wrap leaves tightly around mixture. Line bottom of 3-quart microproof casserole with some leftover cabbage leaves. Place cabbage rolls on top of loose leaves. Cover with remaining cabbage leaves. Dot with butter and pour tomato sauce over top. Cook, covered, on 80 (reheat) about 30 minutes. Baste after 15 minutes, and cook until rolls are fork-tender. Remove and let stand, covered, 5 minutes. Discard top loose cabbage leaves before serving.

6 to 8 servings

Irish Stew →

Chili con Carne
Total Cooking Time: 19 to 22 minutes

1 pound lean ground beef
¼ cup minced onion
½ cup chopped green pepper
1 clove garlic, minced
1 to 2 tablespoons chili
  powder
1 teaspoon salt
1 can (16 ounces) tomatoes,
  chopped and undrained
1 can (16 ounces) kidney
  beans, undrained

Crumble ground beef into 2-quart microproof casserole or baking dish. Add onion, green pepper, and garlic. Cook, uncovered, on HI (max. power) 4 minutes. Drain meat and break up with fork. Add remaining ingredients. Cook, covered, on 70 (roast) 15 to 18 minutes, or until hot. Stir once during cooking time, adjust seasonings. Let stand 5 minutes before serving.

4 servings

All-American Meatballs
Total Cooking Time: 13 to 14 minutes

1 pound lean ground beef
1 medium potato, peeled and
  coarsely grated
2 tablespoons dried onion
  soup mix
1 tablespoon dried parsley
  flakes
1 egg, beaten
2 cups beef broth
1 tablespoon Worcestershire
  sauce
2 tablespoons cornstarch
2 tablespoons water

Combine ground beef, potato, onion soup mix, parsley flakes, and egg in large mixing bowl. Shape into 12 (1½-inch) meatballs; set aside. In a 2-quart microproof casserole, mix beef broth and Worcestershire. Add meatballs. Cook, covered, on 70 (roast) 10 minutes. Combine cornstarch and water in small bowl until smooth; stir into meatballs and cover. Cook on 70 (roast) 3 to 4 minutes, or until sauce is thickened (200° if using probe). Let stand, covered, 5 minutes before serving.

4 servings

Tomato Swiss Steak
Total Cooking Time: 55 minutes

¼ cup all-purpose flour
1 teaspoon salt
¼ teaspoon pepper
1½ to 2 pounds round steak,
  ½ inch thick
2 large onions, sliced
1 green pepper, cut in
  strips
2 cans (6 ounces) tomato
  paste
1 can (10¾ ounces) beef
  broth

Combine flour, salt, and pepper. Place steak on cutting board; pound half of the flour mixture into each side of steak with meat mallet or edge of saucer. Cut meat into 4 pieces and place in 8-inch round or 11 × 7-inch microproof baking dish. Sprinkle remaining flour mixture over meat. Spread onions, green pepper, and tomato paste over meat. Pour in broth, to cover meat. Cover with waxed paper, cook on HI (max. power) 5 minutes. Cook on 60 (bake) 40 minutes. Rearrange meat. Cook on 60 (bake) 10 minutes, or until meat is tender.

4 servings

The ingredients in this recipe may be cut in half for 2 servings. Cut the cooking time to 3 minutes on HI (max. power) and 30 minutes on 60 (bake).

Zucchini Lasagna
Total Cooking Time: 26 to 31 minutes

Place zucchini in 1½-quart microproof baking dish. Add water. Cook, covered, on HI (max. power) 6 to 7 minutes. Drain and set aside. Crumble beef into 2-quart glass mixing bowl. Cook on HI (max. power) 4 minutes, stirring halfway through cooking time. Pour off drippings. Combine tomato sauce, mushrooms, onion, garlic, basil, oregano, thyme, salt, and pepper. Cook on HI (max. power) 6 to 8 minutes. Stir halfway through cooking time. Layer one-third of zucchini in 11 × 7 × 1½-inch microproof baking dish. Sprinkle with 1 tablespoon of bread crumbs and top with one-third of meat mixture and one-half of cottage cheese and mozzarella. Repeat for second layer, ending with layer of zucchini topped with remaining meat mixture and bread crumbs. Sprinkle with Parmesan cheese. Cover with waxed paper and cook on HI (max. power) 10 to 12 minutes, rotating dish one-quarter turn halfway through cooking time. Let stand, covered, 5 to 10 minutes before serving.

8 to 10 servings

This recipe is a low-calorie noodleless variation of Neapolitan Lasagna on page 131.

6	cups sliced zucchini
¼	cup water
1	pound lean ground beef
2	cans (8 ounces each) tomato sauce
¼	pound mushrooms, chopped
1	small onion, minced
1	clove garlic, minced
1	teaspoon basil
½	teaspoon oregano
½	teaspoon thyme
½	teaspoon salt
¼	teaspoon pepper
¼	cup bread crumbs, divided
12	ounces dry or low-fat, drained cottage cheese
4	ounces shredded mozzarella cheese
⅓	cup Parmesan cheese, grated

Favorite Meatloaf
Total Cooking Time: 12 to 14 minutes

In small bowl, combine tomato sauce, brown sugar, and mustard. Set aside. In large mixing bowl, combine eggs, onion, cracker crumbs, ground beef, salt, and pepper. Add ½ cup of tomato sauce mixture and stir thoroughly. Place meat mixture in glass ring mold, or 2-quart microproof round casserole. Pour remaining tomato sauce over top of meat. Cook, uncovered, on HI (max. power) 12 to 14 minutes. Let stand, covered, 5 to 10 minutes before serving.

6 servings

Temperature probe may be used. Insert in center portion of meatloaf. Set at 160°. Let stand before serving, as above. (Garnish with mushrooms for a special treat.)

1	can (8 ounces) tomato sauce, divided
¼	cup brown sugar
1	teaspoon prepared mustard
2	eggs, lightly beaten
1	medium onion, minced
¼	cup cracker crumbs
2	pounds lean ground beef
1½	teaspoons salt
¼	teaspoon pepper

Eggplant Parthenon

Total Cooking Time: 18 minutes

Wash eggplants and cut in half lengthwise. Scoop out insides, leaving a 1-inch-thick shell. Chop eggplant pulp in medium chunks, and set aside. Place onions in 1½-quart microproof casserole. Crumble in lamb. Cook, covered, on HI (max. power) 5 minutes, or just until lamb loses pink color. Drain fat. Dissolve bouillon cube in hot water. Stir bouillon into cooked lamb with ½ cup of tomato sauce and chopped eggplant pulp. Cook, covered, on HI (max. power) 5 minutes, stirring occasionally. Remove from oven, stir in oregano, cinnamon, parsley, salt, and pepper. Fill eggplant halves with mixture. Sprinkle bread crumbs over top. Drizzle remaining tomato sauce over top of crumbs. Place in 11 × 7-inch oval microproof baking dish. Cover with waxed paper, cook on 80 (reheat) 8 minutes, or just until eggplant is tender.

4 servings

2 medium eggplants
2 medium onions, chopped
1 pound ground lamb
1 beef bouillon cube
½ cup hot water
1 can (8 ounces) tomato sauce, divided
½ teaspoon oregano
¼ teaspoon cinnamon
2 tablespoons chopped parsley
½ teaspoon salt
¼ teaspoon pepper
½ cup dry bread crumbs

Stuffed Green Peppers

Total Cooking Time: 16 to 18 minutes

Wash peppers, remove tops and seeds. Place upright in 2-quart microproof casserole. Pour water over bottom of dish and cook, covered, on HI (max. power) 2 minutes. Drain water. Let peppers stand while preparing filling. Crumble beef into glass mixing bowl. Add onion and cook on HI (max. power) 4 minutes, or until meat loses its color, stirring once during cooking. Drain fat. Stir in garlic, salt, pepper, rice, parsley, and ½ cup of tomato sauce. Fill green peppers with mixture, mounding on top. Replace peppers in casserole and top each with remaining tomato sauce. Cook, covered, on HI (max. power) 10 to 12 minutes, or until peppers are tender.

4 servings

4 large green peppers
¼ cup water
1 pound lean ground beef
1 medium onion, finely chopped
1 clove garlic, minced
1 teaspoon salt
¼ teaspoon pepper
1½ cups cooked rice
1 tablespoon minced fresh parsley
1 can (8 ounces) tomato sauce, divided

This recipe may easily be cut in half for two servings.

← *Eggplant Parthenon, Stuffed Green Peppers, Eggs in Nests (page 123)*

Veal Parmigiana
Total Cooking Time: 15 to 17 minutes

1 egg
¼ teaspoon salt
3 tablespoons cracker crumbs
⅓ cup grated Parmesan cheese
4 veal cutlets, about 1 pound
2 tablespoons vegetable oil
¼ cup dry vermouth
1 medium onion, minced
1 cup (4 ounces) shredded
  mozzarella cheese
1 can (8 ounces) tomato sauce
⅛ teaspoon pepper
⅛ teaspoon oregano

Beat egg and salt in shallow dish. Combine cracker crumbs and Parmesan cheese on waxed paper square. Place each veal cutlet between 2 pieces of waxed paper and pound with smooth-surfaced meat mallet until ¼ inch thick. Dip veal in egg, then in cracker crumbs, and set aside. Preheat 9-inch microwave browning dish 7 minutes on HI (max. power), adding vegetable oil after preheating. Brown 2 veal cutlets at a time as follows: Lay cutlets on dish, cover with waxed paper, and cook on HI (max. power) 1½ to 2 minutes. Turn and cook on HI (max. power) 1 to 1½ minutes. Remove and set aside. Brown second 2 cutlets in same manner. Then, arrange all 4 cutlets in browning dish. Add vermouth, sprinkle onion over meat, top with cheese, then sauce, and season with pepper and oregano. Cook, covered, on 60 (bake) 10 minutes, or until sauce is hot and cheese melted.

4 servings

Alternate method: If you do not have a browning dish, brown cutlets in skillet on top of stove. When brown, transfer to a 8 or 9-inch microproof baking dish and add remaining ingredients as in directions above. Cook, covered, on 60 (bake) for 10 minutes. They are delicious!

Country Style Ribs
Total Cooking Time: 55 to 60 minutes

2½ to 3 pounds country-style
  pork ribs
½ cup Spicy Barbecue Sauce
  (page 158)
3 tablespoons olive oil
1 tablespoon wine vinegar
1 tablespoon chopped onion
1 teaspoon chopped fresh
  parsley
½ teaspoon salt
⅛ teaspoon pepper
1 clove garlic, minced

Place ribs in 3-quart (13×9×2-inch) glass baking dish, cover with waxed paper. Cook on 70 (roast) 25 minutes; after 15 minutes, rearrange by placing outside ribs in center. Drain off fat. Mix remaining ingredients well and brush over both sides of ribs. Cook, covered on 70 (roast) 30 to 35 minutes, or until meat is fork tender. Let stand, covered, 5 minutes before serving.

4 to 6 servings

If you are in a hurry, substitute ½ cup bottled barbecue sauce for the homemade barbecue sauce, and ¼ cup bottled Italian dressing for the oil, vinegar, salt, and pepper.

Veal Cordon Bleu

Total Cooking Time: 4½ minutes

½ pound veal cutlets,
   ½ inch thick
1 slice Swiss cheese
2 thin slices boiled ham
1½ tablespoons all-purpose
   flour
1 egg
1 tablespoon water
¼ cup dry bread crumbs
1½ tablespoons butter or
   margarine
1 tablespoon chopped fresh
   parsley
2 tablespoons dry vermouth

Cut veal into 4 pieces. Place each piece of veal between 2 sheets of waxed paper and pound with smooth-surfaced meat mallet until veal is ⅛ inch thick. Cut cheese in 2 pieces, then fold each piece in half. Place on slice of ham. Roll ham around cheese three times so that finished roll of ham is smaller than the pieces of veal. Place rolled ham on 1 slice of veal and top with second slice. Press edges of veal together to seal. Repeat for second portion. Place flour on piece of waxed paper. Beat egg lightly with water. Place bread crumbs on piece of waxed paper. Dip veal sandwiches in flour, then in beaten egg; finally, coat well with bread crumbs. Place butter and parsley in an 8-inch microproof baking dish. Cook on HI (max. power) 30 seconds, or just long enough to heat butter well. Add veal sandwiches to very hot butter. Cook, uncovered, on HI (max. power) 4 minutes, turning veal over after 2 minutes. Remove veal, add wine to butter remaining in pan. Blend, pour over veal, and serve immediately.

2 servings

Sweet and Sour Pork

Total Cooking Time: 19 minutes

1 can (16 ounces) pineapple
   chunks
4 medium carrots, thinly
   sliced
¼ cup vegetable oil
1 medium onion, sliced
2 green peppers, sliced
2 pounds lean boneless pork,
   cut in ¾-inch cubes
¼ cup cornstarch
½ cup soy sauce
½ cup brown sugar
¼ cup wine vinegar
1 tablespoon Worcestershire
   sauce
¼ teaspoon hot-pepper sauce
½ teaspoon pepper

Drain pineapple chunks, reserving ½ cup syrup. Set aside. Place carrots and oil in 3-quart microproof casserole. Stir. Cook, covered, on HI (max. power) 4 minutes. Add onion, green peppers, and pork; stir. Cook, covered, on HI (max. power) 5 minutes. Meanwhile, in a bowl, mix reserved pineapple syrup and cornstarch. Stir in remaining ingredients. Add to pork, along with pineapple chunks. Stir. Cook, covered, on HI (max. power) 10 minutes, or until sauce has thickened and pork is done. Serve with rice or chow mein noodles.

8 servings

Julienne of Veal

Total Cooking Time: 15 minutes

Trim veal of all membrane. Place 1 piece of cutlet at a time between 2 pieces waxed paper. Pound with smooth-surfaced mallet or rolling pin until $1/4$ inch thick. Sprinkle meat lightly on each side with salt, paprika, and pepper. Cut into strips $1/4$ inch wide and $1\frac{1}{2}$ inches long. In $11 \times 7 \times 1\frac{1}{2}$-inch microproof baking dish, melt 2 tablespoons butter on HI (max. power) 45 seconds. Stir in onion and mushrooms. Cook on HI (max. power) 3 minutes, stirring once during cooking time. Add veal and cook on 70 (roast) 5 minutes, or until no longer pink. Stir once during cooking time. Lift meat and vegetables from drippings and set aside. Add remaining tablespoon butter to baking dish and stir until melted. Stir in flour and cook on HI (max. power) 1 minute. Stir in wine and cream. Cook, uncovered, on 70 (roast) 3 minutes, or until sauce is smooth and thickened, stirring once during cooking time. Add meat to sauce and cook, uncovered, on 80 (reheat) 2 minutes, or until completely hot. Remove from oven. Put brandy in small microproof cup. Heat, uncovered, on 80 (reheat) 10 to 15 seconds. Remove, ignite, pour over meat, and serve at once.

4 servings

1 pound veal cutlets, $1/2$ inch thick
  Salt, paprika, and pepper
3 tablespoons butter or margarine, divided
2 tablespoons chopped green onion
$1/4$ pound mushrooms, sliced
2 tablespoons all-purpose flour
$1/4$ cup dry white wine
$1/2$ cup heavy cream
2 tablespoons brandy

Ham and Noodle Casserole

Total Cooking Time: 17 to 20 minutes

Cook egg noodles according to chart on page 129. Set aside. In $1\frac{1}{2}$-quart microproof casserole, combine ham, onion, tarragon, and butter. Cook, covered, on HI (max. power) 3 minutes. Add chicken soup, egg noodles, green beans, and water. Stir. Cook, covered, on HI (max. power) 5 minutes, or until hot, stirring once during cooking time. Top with bread crumbs. Let stand, covered, 2 to 3 minutes before serving.

4 servings

Fresh, frozen, or canned green beans may be used. The canned beans need not be precooked, simply drain.

---

1 cup uncooked fine egg noodles
$1\frac{1}{2}$ cups diced cooked ham
2 tablespoons chopped onion
$1/8$ teaspoon tarragon
2 tablespoons butter or margarine
1 can ($10\frac{1}{2}$ ounces) condensed cream of chicken soup, undiluted
$1/2$ cup French-style green beans, precooked and drained
$1/2$ cup water
2 tablespoons bread crumbs

Barbecued Spareribs

Total Cooking Time: 36 to 38 minutes

Cut spareribs into individual ribs. Arrange in large microproof baking dish. Cook, covered with waxed paper, on 70 (roast) 28 minutes. Turn over and rearrange halfway through cooking. Drain off fat. In small bowl mix together remaining ingredients. Generously spoon sauce on ribs. Cook, covered, on 70 (roast) 8 to 10 minutes. Let stand 10 minutes before serving.

4 servings

2 to 2½ pounds fresh pork spareribs
2 tablespoons instant onion flakes
1 can (8 ounces) tomato sauce
1 tablespoon lemon juice
1 tablespoon brown sugar
1 teaspoon Worcestershire sauce
1 teaspoon prepared mustard
½ teaspoon salt
¼ teaspoon pepper
¼ teaspoon hot-pepper sauce

Baked Ham with Pineapple

Total Cooking Time: 28 to 29 minutes

Place ham, fat side down, on shallow microproof baking dish. Cook on 70 (roast) 21 minutes. Turn ham over. Drain pineapple, reserving juice. Combine 2 teaspoons of juice with brown sugar to make paste. Spread over top of ham. Put pineapple slices on top and stud with cloves. Attach pineapple with toothpicks if necessary. Cook on 70 (roast) 7 to 8 minutes. Let stand, covered with aluminum foil, about 10 minutes before serving.

8 to 10 servings

1 3-pound precooked ham
1 can (4 ounces) pineapple slices
¼ cup brown sugar
Whole cloves

Orange Ginger Pork Chops

Total Cooking Time: 22 minutes

Trim fat from pork chops. Place in oblong microproof baking dish. Pour orange juice over chops. Cover with waxed paper; cook on 70 (roast) 12 minutes. Turn chops over, sprinkle with salt, garlic powder, and ginger. Place slice of orange peel on top of each chop. Cook, covered, on HI (max. power) 10 minutes. Top each chop with spoonful of sour cream and let stand, covered, 5 minutes before serving.

6 servings

6 lean pork loin chops
¼ cup orange juice
½ teaspoon salt
½ teaspoon garlic powder
2 teaspoons ground ginger
6 slices orange peel
½ cup dairy sour cream

← *Barbecued Spareribs*

Stuffed Pork Chops

Total Cooking Time: 14¾ to 18¾ minutes

2 tablespoons melted butter
or margarine
1 cup coarse dry bread crumbs
½ cup chopped apple
2 tablespoons chopped raisins
½ teaspoon salt
2 tablespoons sugar
2 tablespoons minced onion
¼ teaspoon pepper
Pinch sage
2 tablespoons hot water
8 thin pork loin chops
½ package (⅜ ounce) brown
gravy mix

In 4-cup glass measure melt butter on HI (max. power) 45 seconds. Add bread crumbs, apple, raisins, salt, sugar, onion, pepper, and sage, mixing lightly. Moisten slightly with hot water. Trim all fat from pork chops. Place 4 chops in bottom of 8-inch microproof baking dish. Divide stuffing into 4 portions; place 1 portion on top of each chop. Cover chops with 4 remaining chops, pressing together lightly. Sprinkle brown gravy mix over top of chops — to make an even layer, sift mixture through small strainer. Cover with waxed paper and cook on 70 (roast) 14 to 18 minutes, or just until done. Let stand 5 minutes before serving.

4 servings

Herbed Leg of Lamb

Total Cooking Time: 24 to 48 minutes

3 to 4-pound butterflied lamb
leg roast boneless
2 cloves garlic
1 tablespoon dry mustard
1 teaspoon salt
⅛ teaspoon pepper
½ teaspoon thyme
¼ teaspoon rosemary
1 teaspoon lemon juice
1½ tablespoons soy sauce

Rub all surfaces of lamb with one of the garlic cloves, peeled and halved. Then cut both cloves into slivers. Slit outside of lamb at intervals and insert sliced garlic into slits. Mix the mustard, salt, pepper, thyme, rosemary, lemon juice, and soy sauce. Spread over both sides of lamb. Place on microproof meat rack in shallow baking dish. Cook, covered loosely with waxed paper, on 70 (roast) 8 to 10 minutes per pound for medium and 10 to 12 minutes per pound for well done. Let stand 10 minutes before slicing.

6 to 8 servings

Zesty Lamb Chops

Total Cooking Time: 20 minutes

4 shoulder lamb chops
½ cup coarsely chopped onion
1 clove garlic, minced
½ cup catsup
2 tablespoons Worcestershire
sauce
1 tablespoon prepared mustard

In microproof baking dish arrange lamb chops in one layer. Sprinkle with onion and garlic. Cook, covered, on HI (max. power) 5 minutes. Combine remaining ingredients and spread over lamb chops. Cover with waxed paper and cook on 60 (bake) 15 minutes, or until lamb chops are tender.

4 servings

Stuffed Pork Chops →

Lamb Ragout
Total Cooking Time: 40 to 45 minutes

1 pound lamb for stew
   cut in 1-inch
   cubes
1 package (⅝ ounce) brown
   gravy mix
2 tablespoons all-purpose
   flour
1 teaspoon salt
⅛ teaspoon pepper
1 clove garlic, minced
½ teaspoon Worcestershire
   sauce
¼ cup dry red wine
3 medium carrots, cut in
   chunks
2 stalks celery, cut in
   chunks
2 potatoes, peeled and cubed
1 cup water

In 3-quart microproof casserole, combine lamb and gravy mix. Cook, uncovered, on 70 (roast) 10 minutes, stirring once during cooking time. Add remaining ingredients. Stir well. Cook, covered, on 50 (simmer) 30 to 35 minutes, or until meat and vegetables are tender. Stir once during cooking time. Let stand 3 to 4 minutes before serving.

4 servings

The ingredients in this lamb stew may easily be cut in half for two servings. For best results, use 2 thin carrots. Cook lamb and gravy mix 10 minutes as above. After remaining ingredients are added, cook on 50 (simmer) 18 to 20 minutes.

Liver Venetian Style
Total Cooking Time: 16 to 19 minutes

4 slices bacon
2 medium onions, thinly
   sliced
1 pound sliced calves liver
   Salt and pepper

Place bacon slices in 10-inch microproof pie plate. Cover with paper towels and cook on HI (max. power) 3 to 4 minutes, or until crisp. Remove bacon, reserving drippings; drain bacon on paper towels. Add onions to drippings, stir to coat them. Cover with paper towels and cook on HI (max. power) 5 minutes, or until onions are transparent. Move onions to side of dish and add liver. Turn to coat both sides with drippings. Cover with waxed paper and cook on 70 (roast) 8 to 10 minutes, or until no longer pink. Season with salt and pepper. Serve liver topped with onions and crumbled bacon.

4 servings

Chicken, turkey, duck, and Cornish hen are especially juicy, tender, and flavorful when cooked in a microwave oven. Because they require less attention than other meats, they are great favorites for microwave cooks on those days when too many things seem to be happening at once. Poultry turns out golden brown but not crisp. If you have crisp-skin lovers at your table, you can satisfy them by crisping the skin in a conventional oven at 450°, after the microwave cooking. You can also avoid the frustrations of long barbecue cooking by partially cooking poultry in the microwave oven, then finishing it off on the charcoal grill. Try the tasty recipes suggested here and then adapt your own. You'll even want to experiment with new recipes when you discover how much easier it is to cook poultry in your microwave oven than in the conventional oven.

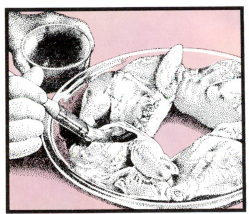

A browning sauce may be brushed on poultry before cooking if you prefer a more-browned appearance than the microwave normally provides (above left). The best arrangement for chicken parts (above). Turning Microwave Fried Chicken (page 98) in a browning dish (left).

Converting Your Recipes

Conventional one-dish poultry recipes that call for cut-up pieces are easy to adapt for the microwave. The temperature probe can help achieve accurate doneness in whole-chicken recipes as well as in casseroles. Refer to the comparative chicken recipes on page 36 to guide you in converting your favorite dishes. Here are some good tips to follow:

☐ To obtain uniform doneness and flavor, cook poultry weighing no more than 14 pounds in the microwave oven. Poultry over 14 pounds should be cooked conventionally.

☐ Butter- or oil-injected turkeys often have uneven concentrations of fat and thus cook unevenly. For best results, use uninjected turkeys.

☐ Conventional pop-up indicators for doneness do not work correctly in the microwave.

☐ The temperature probe may be used in cooking whole poultry. Insert the probe in the fleshy part of the inside thigh muscle without touching the bone.

☐ Poultry pieces prepared in a cream sauce should be cooked on 70 (roast) to prevent the cream from separating or curdling.

☐ Chicken coated with a crumb mixture cooks to crispness more easily if left uncovered.

☐ Less tender game birds should be cooked on 70 (roast) on a microwave roasting rack. Pour off fat as necessary. For best results, marinate game birds before cooking.

☐ Standing time is essential to complete cooking. Allow up to 15 minutes standing time for whole poultry depending upon size. The internal temperature will rise approximately 15° during 15 minutes standing time. Chicken pieces and casseroles need only 5 minutes standing time.

Using the Defrosting Guide

1. Poultry can be defrosted within the original paper or plastic wrapping. Remove all metal rings, wire twist ties, and any aluminum foil. Since it is difficult to remove metal clamps from legs of frozen turkey, the clamps need not be removed until after defrosting. Be careful, of course, that the metal is at least 1 inch from the oven walls.

2. Place poultry in microproof dish while defrosting.

3. Defrost only as long as necessary.

Poultry should be cool in the center when removed from the oven.

4. To speed defrosting during standing time, poultry may be placed in a cold-water bath.

5. Separate cut-up chicken pieces as soon as partially thawed.

6. Wing and leg tips and area near breast bone may begin cooking before center is thoroughly defrosted. As soon as these areas appear thawed, cover them with small strips of aluminum foil; this foil should be at least 1 inch from oven walls.

DEFROSTING GUIDE — POULTRY

Food	Amount	Minutes (per pound)	Cook Control Setting	Standing Time (in minutes)	Special Notes
Capon	6-8 lbs.	2	70 (roast)	60	Turn over once. Immerse in cold water for standing time.
Chicken, cut up	2-3 lbs.	5-6	30 (defrost)	10-15	Turn every 5 minutes. Separate pieces when partially thawed.
Chicken, whole	2-3 lbs.	6-8	30 (defrost)	25-30	Turn over once. Immerse in cold water for standing time.
Cornish hens	1, 1-1½ lbs. 2, 1-1½ lbs. ea.	6-8 8-10	30 (defrost) 30 (defrost)	20 20	Turn over once.
Duckling	4-5 lbs.	4	70 (roast)	30-40	Turn over once. Immerse in cold water for standing time.
Turkey	Under 8 lbs. Over 8 lbs.	3-5 3-5	30 (defrost) 70 (roast)	60 60	Turn over once. Immerse in cold water for standing time.
Turkey breast	Under 4 lbs. Over 4 lbs.	3-5 1 2	30 (defrost) 70 (roast) 50 (simmer)	20 20	Turn over once. Start at 70 (roast), turn over, continue on 50 (simmer).
Turkey drumsticks	1-1½ lbs.	5-6	30 (defrost)	15-20	Turn every 5 minutes. Separate pieces when partially thawed.
Turkey roast, boneless	2-4 lbs.	3-4	30 (defrost)	10	Remove from foil pan. Cover with waxed paper.

Using the Cooking Guide

1. Defrost frozen poultry completely before cooking.
2. Remove the giblets, rinse poultry in cool water, and pat dry.
3. Brush poultry with browning sauce before cooking.
4. When cooking whole birds, place on a microproof roasting rack in a glass baking dish large enough to catch drippings.
5. Turn over, as directed in Guide, halfway through cooking time.
6. Cook whole poultry covered loosely with a waxed paper tent to prevent splattering. Toward end of cooking time, small pieces of aluminum foil may be used for shielding to cover legs, wing tips, or breast bone area to prevent over cooking. Foil should be at least 1 inch from oven walls.
7. Cover poultry pieces with either glass lid or plastic wrap during cooking and standing time.
8. Use temperature probe inserted in thickest part of thigh, set at 180° for whole poultry, and at 170° for parts, including turkey breasts.
9. Standing time completes the cooking of poultry. Cooked whole birds may be covered with aluminum foil during standing time.

COOKING GUIDE — POULTRY

Food	First Cook Control Setting and Time (in minutes)	Second Cook Control Setting and Time (in minutes)	or	Temperature Probe Setting	Standing Time (in minutes)	Special Notes
Chicken, whole, 2-3 pounds	HI (max. power) 3-4 per pound	Turn over. HI (max. power) 4 per pound	or	Turn over. 180°	5 (covered with foil)	Shallow baking dish, roasting rack, breast up.
3-5 pounds	HI (max. power) 4 per pound	Turn over. HI (max. power) 4-5 per pound	or	Turn over. 180°	5	12×7-inch baking dish, roasting rack, breast up.
Chicken, cut up 2½-3½ pounds	HI (max. power) 10	Turn over. HI (max. power) 8-12	or	Turn over. 170°	5	12×7-inch baking dish. Cover.
Chicken, quartered	HI (max. power) 3-4 per pound	Turn over. HI (max. power) 3-4 per pound	or	Turn over. 170°	5	Shallow baking dish, skin side down.
Cornish hens 1-1½ pounds	HI (max. power) 4 per pound	Turn over. HI (max. power) 3 per pound	or	Turn over. 180°	5	Shallow baking dish, breast down. Cover.
Duckling 4-5 pounds	70 (roast) 4 per pound	Turn over. Drain excess fat. 70 (roast) 4 per pound	or	Turn over. 170°	8-10	Shallow baking dish, roasting rack. Cover.
Turkey, whole, 8-14 pounds	HI (max. power) 5 per pound	Turn over. 70 (roast) 4 per pound	or	Turn over. 70 (roast) 180°	10-15 (covered with foil)	Shallow baking dish, 13×9-inch, roasting rack, breast up.
Turkey breast, 3-4 pounds	HI (max. power) 7 per pound	Turn over. 70 (roast) 5 per pound	or	Turn over. 70 (roast) 170°		Shallow baking dish, roasting rack.
Turkey roast, boneless 2-4 pounds	70 (roast) 10 per pound	Turn over. 70 (roast) 9 per pound	or	Turn over. 70 (roast) 170°	10-15	Loaf pan. Cover with plastic wrap.
Turkey parts, 2-3 pounds	70 (roast) 7-8 per pound	Turn over. 70 (roast) 7-8 per pound			5	Shallow baking dish with roasting rack.

Easy Baked Chicken
Total Cooking Time: 15 to 17 minutes

1 broiler-fryer chicken,
  2½ to 3 pounds
  Salt and pepper
1 small onion, quartered
2 stalks celery, cut in
  1-inch slices
2 tablespoons soft butter
  or margarine
⅛ teaspoon thyme

Remove giblets, wash chicken, and pat dry. Sprinkle inside of body cavity with salt and pepper. Place onion and celery inside body cavity. Tie legs together with string and tie wings to body. Place chicken, breast side up, on a microwave roasting rack in a 12×7×2-inch microproof baking dish. Spread with soft butter and sprinkle with thyme. Cook on HI (max. power) 15 to 17 minutes, or until done. Let stand, covered with aluminum foil, about 5 minutes before serving.

4 servings

COOKING GUIDE — CONVENIENCE POULTRY

Food	Amount	Cook Control Setting	Time (in Minutes)	Special Notes
Precooked breaded chicken, frozen	1 piece 2 pieces 4 pieces 2 - 3 lbs.	80 (reheat)	1 - 1½ 2 - 2½ 2½ - 3 10 - 12	Remove wrapping and place in microproof baking dish.
Chicken Kiev, frozen	1 piece 2 pieces	30 (defrost) HI (max. power) 30 (defrost) HI (max. power)	4 - 5 2½ - 3 6 - 7 4 - 5	Remove plastic wrap, place on microproof plate. First, thaw on 30 (defrost) and then, cook on HI (max. power).
Chicken à la King, frozen	5 oz.	HI (max. power)	3 - 4	Place on microproof plate. Stir before serving.
Creamed Chicken, Chicken and Dumplings, canned	7½ - 10½ oz.	80 (reheat)	2 - 4	Stir once. You may use temperature probe at 150° on 80 (reheat) for canned poultry.
Escalloped chicken, chow mein, canned	14 - 24 oz.	80 (reheat)	4 - 6	Stir halfway through cooking time.
Turkey tetrazzini, frozen	12 oz.	HI (max. power)	3 - 4	Place on microproof plate. Stir before serving.
Turkey, sliced in gravy, frozen	5 oz.	HI (max. power)	3 - 5	Place in microproof dish. Make slit in pouch before heating.

Chicken Supreme
Total Cooking Time: 46 to 52 minutes

Cook bacon according to directions on page 71. Crumble and set aside. Mix soup, wine, onion, garlic, bouillon, and seasonings in small bowl. Place carrots and potatoes in bottom of 3-quart microproof casserole. Arrange chicken pieces on top, placing thicker portions around outside of dish and chicken wings in center. Pour soup mixture over top. Cook, covered, on HI (max. power) 30 minutes. Sprinkle mushrooms and crumbled bacon on top. Cook, covered on 70 (roast) 10 to 15 minutes. Let stand 5 minutes before serving.

4 to 6 servings

For 2 or 3 servings, use 14 to 16 ounces (3 pieces) cut-up chicken, and halve the rest of the ingredients. Cut chicken and vegetable cooking time to 20 to 25 minutes on HI (max. power).

5 slices bacon
1 can (10¾ ounces) cream of onion soup, undiluted
½ cup dry red wine or dry sherry
½ cup chopped onion
1 clove garlic, minced
1½ teaspoons instant chicken bouillon
1 tablespoon minced fresh parsley
½ teaspoon salt
¼ teaspoon thyme
¼ teaspoon pepper
2 medium carrots, sliced thin
6 small potatoes, peeled and halved
1 frying chicken, 2½ to 3 pounds, cut up
8 ounces mushrooms, sliced

Chicken Cacciatore

Total Cooking Time: 34 to 40 minutes

In a 3-quart microproof casserole, combine onion, green pepper, and butter. Cook, covered, on HI (max. power) 4 to 5 minutes, or until onion is transparent. Add tomatoes and flour, stir until smooth. Stir in all remaining ingredients except chicken. Cook, covered, on HI (max. power) 5 minutes. Add chicken pieces, immersing them in sauce. Cook, covered, on HI (max. power) 20 to 25 minutes, or until chicken is tender. Stir once during cooking. Allow to stand 5 minutes, covered. Remove bay leaf before serving with cooked spaghetti or rice.

4 to 6 servings

1 medium onion, chopped
1 medium green pepper, thinly sliced
1 tablespoon butter or margarine
1 can (28 ounces) whole tomatoes
$1/4$ cup all-purpose flour
1 bay leaf
1 tablespoon dried parsley flakes
1 teaspoon salt
1 clove garlic, minced
$1/2$ teaspoon oregano
1 teaspoon paprika
$1/4$ teaspoon pepper
$1/4$ teaspoon basil
$1/2$ cup dry red wine or water
1 frying chicken, $2\frac{1}{2}$ to 3 pounds, cut up

Tarragon Grilled Chicken

Total Cooking Time: 18 to 22 minutes

Combine all ingredients except chicken. Arrange chicken pieces skin side down with thick edges toward outside of 12-inch oval microproof baking dish. Brush chicken with half the oil mixture. Cook, covered with waxed paper, on HI (max. power) 10 minutes. Turn chicken and brush generously with remaining oil mixture. Cook, covered, on HI (max. power) 8 to 12 minutes. Let stand 5 minutes before serving.

4 servings

$1/4$ cup olive oil
$1/4$ cup dry sherry or chicken broth
1 tablespoon onion flakes
1 clove garlic, minced
1 teaspoon salt
$1/2$ teaspoon tarragon
$1/8$ teaspoon white pepper
1 broiler-fryer chicken, $2\frac{1}{2}$ to 3 pounds, quartered

This chicken dish is delicious when finished on the charcoal grill. First cook chicken in microwave oven 8 minutes on one side, and 7 to 9 minutes on the other, or until nearly done. Reserve juices and oil mixture remaining in microproof dish. Barbecue about 4 inches above hot coals for 10 to 12 minutes, or until golden brown. Turn occasionally and brush with reserved juices and oil mixture.

Microwave Fried Chicken
Total Cooking Time: 10½ minutes

½ cup flour
½ teaspoon salt
¼ teaspoon pepper
⅛ teaspoon dry mustard
1 frying chicken (2½ to 3 pounds), cut up, back and wing tips removed
2 tablespoons lemon juice
2 tablespoons cooking oil
2 tablespoons butter
Paprika

In paper bag, combine flour, salt, pepper, and mustard; shake well. Brush chicken pieces with lemon juice. Place a few pieces of chicken at a time in paper bag, shake until coated. Remove chicken from bag, lightly shake pieces free of excess flour. Preheat 9-inch browning dish on HI (max. power) 4½ minutes. Add oil and butter, arrange chicken (skin side down) without crowding. Cover loosely with waxed paper. Cook on HI (max. power) 3 minutes. Turn chicken, sprinkle with paprika. Cook on HI (max. power) 3 minutes. Let stand, covered with aluminum foil, about 5 minutes before serving.

8 to 10 servings

If more browning is preferred, preheat conventional oven to broil, watch carefully. Fine bread crumbs may be substituted for flour in coating.

Quick Brunswick Stew
Total Cooking Time: 24 to 26 minutes

1 package (10 ounces) frozen whole-kernel corn
2 tablespoons vegetable oil
2 small chicken breasts, (1½ pounds) split
4 chicken thighs
1 can (10¾ ounces) condensed chicken gumbo soup
1½ teaspoons Worcestershire sauce
¼ teaspoon salt
⅛ teaspoon pepper
1 clove garlic, minced

Defrost corn in package on HI (max. power) 3 minutes, set aside. Preheat 9-inch browning dish on HI (max. power) 6 minutes. Add oil; cook chicken on HI (max. power) 1 to 2 minutes per side, or until brown. Place in one layer in 12×7×2-inch microproof baking dish, skin side down, with thicker portions at the outer edge of dish. Mix all other ingredients, including corn, in small bowl. Pour mixture over chicken. Cover with waxed paper. Cook on HI (max. power) 8 minutes. Turn chicken and spoon sauce on top. Cook, covered, on HI (max. power) 8 minutes. Allow to stand, covered, 5 minutes before serving.

4 servings

Serve with Dandy Dumplings (page 160). You can parboil them for 6 minutes as the recipe directs and then finish the dumplings off by adding them to the stew during the last 8 minutes of cooking time.

Microwave Fried Chicken →

Soy Sherry Chicken
Total Cooking Time: 24 to 30 minutes

1 small onion, halved
1 broiler-fryer chicken,
    2½ to 3 pounds
¼ cup soy sauce
¼ cup dry sherry
3 slices fresh ginger
    (⅛ inch thick)

Place onion in cavity of chicken. Brush skin with soy sauce and place chicken, breast up, in cooking bag. Add sherry, any remaining soy sauce, and ginger to bag. Close bag with string or rubber band. Place on microproof baking dish. Pierce bag near closure. Insert temperature probe into thickest part of inner thigh parallel to leg. Cook on 80 (reheat) set at 180°. Let stand 10 minutes before serving. Discard onion and ginger slices.

4 servings

If not using the probe, cook in bag on 80 (reheat) 8 to 10 minutes per pound, or until done. This dish has reduced calories if you substitute chicken bouillon for sherry.

Barbecued Chicken
Total Cooking Time: 18 to 20 minutes

1 broiler-fryer chicken,
    2½ pounds, quartered
½ cup Spicy Barbecue Sauce
    (page 158)
1 tablespoon dried parsley
    flakes
1 tablespoon onion flakes

Arrange chicken pieces, skin side down, with thick edges toward outside of 12 × 7 × 2-inch microproof baking dish. Combine remaining ingredients. Brush half the sauce over top of chicken. Cook, covered with waxed paper, on HI (max. power) 10 minutes. Turn chicken, brush with remaining sauce. Cook, covered, on HI (max. power) 8 to 10 minutes, or until chicken is tender. Let stand, covered, 5 minutes before serving.

4 servings

Swiss Coated Chicken
Total Cooking Time: 4½ minutes

1 large chicken breast
    (1 pound), split, boned,
    and skinned
¼ teaspoon paprika
¼ teaspoon white pepper
1 teaspoon cornstarch
2 tablespoons apple juice
⅓ cup light cream
½ cup grated Swiss
    cheese
1 tablespoon chopped fresh
    parsley

Place chicken in shallow microproof baking dish. Combine paprika, pepper, and cornstarch, stir in apple juice and cream, and pour over chicken. Cook, covered, on HI (max. power) 1 minute. Stir sauce and turn chicken. Cook, covered, on HI (max. power) 2 minutes; stir. Sprinkle cheese over chicken. Cook, uncovered, on HI (max. power) 1½ minutes, or until cheese melts and chicken is fork-tender. Sprinkle with parsley before serving.

2 servings

Garlic Chicken Italiano

Total Cooking Time: 16 minutes

In shallow microproof casserole, mix oil, garlic, celery, parsley, oregano, salt, pepper, and nutmeg. Add chicken pieces and coat them. Marinate, covered, in refrigerator at least 3 hours. Turn several times during marinating. Cook, covered, on HI (max. power) 8 minutes. Turn chicken over. Cook, covered, on HI (max. power) 8 minutes. Let stand 10 minutes before serving.

4 servings

- ⅓ cup olive oil
- 24 large whole cloves garlic
- 1 stalk celery, thinly sliced
- 2 tablespoons chopped fresh parsley
- ½ teaspoon oregano
- 1 teaspoon salt
- ½ teaspoon pepper
  Pinch ground nutmeg
- 4 chicken legs
- 4 chicken thighs

Chicken Milano

Total Cooking Time: 10 minutes

In medium bowl, mix olive oil, salt, pepper, oregano, and basil. Roll chicken thighs in mixture; let stand, covered, 2 hours in refrigerator. Hold one piece at a time over bowl to drain excess marinade. Set marinade aside; roll chicken in bread crumbs. Place in shallow 9-inch microproof baking dish, skin side down, with thickest portion near edge of dish. Cut ends off potatoes to make quarters even, wipe dry. Roll in remaining marinade, adding more oil if necessary. Place in dish with chicken. Cover with waxed paper; cook on HI (max. power) 5 minutes. Turn chicken, skin side up; turn potatoes over. Sprinkle with paprika. Cook on HI (max. power) 5 minutes. Let stand, covered with aluminum foil, 5 minutes before serving.

4 servings

- 3 tablespoons olive oil
- 1 teaspoon salt
- ½ teaspoon pepper
- ¼ teaspoon oregano
- ¼ teaspoon basil
- 4 large chicken thighs
- 1 cup fine bread crumbs
- 2 medium potatoes, peeled and quartered
  Paprika

Chicken and Vegetables

Total Cooking Time: 20 to 21 minutes

Cut all vegetables into strips 1½ inches long, ¼ inch wide — about 4 cups. Place in shallow 1½-quart microproof dish. Dot with butter and season with salt, pepper and parsley. Cook, covered, with plastic wrap, on HI (max. power) 10 minutes, stirring after 5 minutes. Stir and place 4 chicken pieces around outside of dish on vegetables. Sprinkle chicken with paprika. Cook, covered with plastic wrap, on HI (max. power) 10 to 11 minutes, or until chicken is fork-tender.

4 servings

- 2 small parsnips, peeled
- 2 carrots
- 2 stalks celery
- 1 medium onion
- 2 small potatoes, peeled
- 2 tablespoons butter or margarine
- ½ teaspoon salt
  Dash ground pepper
- 2 tablespoons minced fresh parsley
- 2 chicken breasts (2 pounds), split, boned, and skinned
  Paprika

Heavenly Cornish Hens

Total Cooking Time: 16 to 24 minutes

2 Cornish hens, 1 to 1½
    pounds each
2 tablespoons sherry or water
1 envelope (2⅜ ounces)
    seasoned cooking mix
    for chicken

Wash and split hens lengthwise. Remove backbones and discard. Pat dry. Brush both sides of halves with sherry. Coat with seasoned mix. Place halves breast-side down in 12×7×2-inch microproof baking dish with thickest sides toward outside edge of dish. Cover with waxed paper and cook on HI (max. power) 8 to 12 minutes. Turn hens over, recover, cook on HI (max. power) 8 to 12 minutes, or until fork tender. Let stand 5 minutes before serving.

4 servings

Alternate method: The temperature probe may be used after the hens are turned breast side up. Insert the temperature probe in fleshy part of thigh. Cook on HI (max. power) set at 180°.

What to do with the giblets? Many poultry recipes, of course, don't call for gravy. But make a gravy anyway, using the diced, cooked giblets. Freeze it for those times a gravy would be nice but you've bought chicken pieces without giblets!

Roast Orange Duckling

Total Cooking Time: 36 to 41 minutes

1 fresh or thawed frozen
    duckling, 4 to 5
    pounds
1 orange, peeled and cut in
    chunks
1 medium onion, quartered
½ cup orange marmalade

Remove giblets, wash duckling, and pat dry. Place orange and onion pieces in body cavity. Secure neck skin flap with toothpicks or wooden skewers. Tie legs together and tie wings to body. Place duckling, breast down, on microwave roasting rack in a 12×7×2-inch microproof baking dish. Place marmalade in 1-cup glass measure. Cook on HI (max. power) 1 minute. Spread half the warm marmalade over duckling. Cook on 70 (roast) 20 minutes. Remove from oven and drain off excess fat. Turn breast side up. Brush with remaining marmalade. Cover with waxed paper, cook on 70 (roast) 15 to 20 minutes, or until meat near bone is no longer pink. Let stand, covered with aluminum foil, about 10 minutes before serving.

4 servings

Heavenly Cornish Hens →

Turkey and Nut Stuffing

Total Cooking Time: 1 hour 35 minutes to
1 hour 54 minutes

½ cup butter or margarine
1 cup chicken broth
1 large onion, chopped
2 stalks celery, thinly
    sliced
10 cups day-old bread crumbs
    or ½-inch cubes
1 teaspoon poultry seasoning
¼ cup chopped fresh
    parsley
1 teaspoon salt
1 cup coarsely chopped
    walnuts or pecans
1 fresh or thawed frozen
    turkey, 10 to 12 pounds

Place butter and broth in a 3-quart microproof casserole or baking dish. Add onion and celery. Cook, covered, on 50 (simmer) 5 to 6 minutes. Combine with bread crumbs, poultry seasoning, parsley, salt, and nuts, stir lightly. Wash completely thawed turkey, and pat dry. Stuff neck opening with part of the stuffing. Secure skin flap with strong toothpicks or wooden skewers. Stuff body cavity with remaining stuffing. Tie legs together with strong string. Tie wings tightly to body. Place turkey, breast side down on microwave roasting rack in large microproof baking dish. Cook on HI (max. power) 5 minutes per pound. Drain fat from pan and turn turkey breast side up on rack. Cook, covered with waxed paper tent, on 70 (roast) 4 minutes per pound. Protect thin areas with aluminum foil. Let stand 10 to 15 minutes before carving.

If you like an extra-crisp skin, place turkey in a conventional oven, preheated to 450°, for 10 to 15 minutes, or until desired crispness is reached.

Turkey Tetrazzini

Total Cooking Time: 26 to 34 minutes

4 ounces uncooked spaghetti,
    broken in 2-inch
    lengths
3 tablespoons butter or
    margarine
¼ pound mushrooms, sliced
⅓ cup minced onion
3 tablespoons all-purpose
    flour
2 cups chicken broth
½ cup light cream
¼ cup dry vermouth
½ teaspoon salt
    Dash white pepper
¾ cup grated Parmesan cheese,
    divided
2 cups diced cooked turkey
2 tablespoons minced parsley

Cook spaghetti according to directions on page 129. Drain immediately, rinse in cold water to stop cooking, and set aside. In 3-quart microproof casserole, place butter, mushrooms, and onion. Cook, covered, on 90 (sauté) 3 to 4 minutes, or until onion is transparent. Add flour and stir to form a smooth paste. In 4-cup measure stir together chicken broth, cream, and vermouth. Heat on HI (max. power) 2 minutes. Add to flour mixture, stirring well. Stir in salt, pepper, and ¼ cup of cheese. Mix well. Cook on HI (max. power) 5 to 8 minutes or until mixture comes to a boil and thickens. Stir once during cooking. Add cooked spaghetti, turkey, and remaining cheese, stirring carefully. Cook, covered, on HI (max. power) 2 minutes. Let stand, covered, 5 minutes before serving. Sprinkle with parsley.

6 servings

Poaching and steaming have always been the most classic methods of cooking fish. Now, discover the newest "classic" — fish and shellfish microwave-style! So moist, tender, and delicious that you'll never want to cook seafood any other way. And all this with no elaborate procedures: no need to tie the fish in cheesecloth or use a special fish poacher. Shellfish steam to a succulent tenderness with very little water. If you think your microwave oven cooks chicken and meat fast, you'll be amazed at its speed with fish! For best results, fish should be prepared at the last minute. Even standing time is short. So, when planning a fish dinner have everything ready. *Then* start to cook.

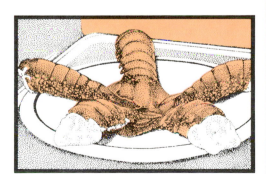

Poached Salmon with Sour Cream Sauce (page 114) is best prepared in an oval baking dish (top left). Oysters Rockefeller (page 115) is a fine entrée or appetizer (top right). Lobster tails are arranged in a circle with the thinnest part at the center of the dish (above left). Stuffed Bass (page 109) with temperature probe inserted (above right).

Converting Your Recipes

If your family likes seafood only when it is fried crackly-crisp, surprise them with a new taste delight when you try traditional fish recipes cooked in the microwave oven. They'll swear fish has been pampered and poached by the most famous French chef. Use the cooking charts and the recipes as guides for adapting your own dishes. If you don't find a recipe that matches or comes close to the conventional recipe you want to adapt, follow this general rule of thumb: Begin cooking at 70 (roast) or at HI (max. power) for one fifth of the time the conventional recipe recommends. Observe, and if it appears to be done earlier, touch "stop" and check. If the dish is not done, continue cooking 30 seconds at a time. As in conventional cooking, the secret to seafood is to watch it carefully, since fish can overcook in seconds. It's best to remove it when barely done and allow standing time to finish the cooking. If you read these simple tips, you'll have excellent results:

☐ Most recipes that specify a particular variety of fish will work when any white fish is substituted. When a recipe calls for fresh or thawed frozen fish fillets, use sole, flounder, bluefish, cod, scrod, or any similar fish.

☐ Cook fish covered unless it is coated with crumbs, which seal in the juices.

☐ When cooking whole fish, the dish should be rotated one-quarter turn twice during the cooking process to help provide even cooking. The odd shape of the fish requires this procedure.

☐ Fish is done when the flesh becomes opaque and barely flakes with a fork.

☐ Shellfish is done when flesh is opaque and just firm.

☐ Shellfish come in their own cooking containers which respond well to microwaves. Clam and mussel shells open before your eyes. Shrimp, crab, and lobster shells turn pink.

☐ All seafood recipes freeze well except where otherwise noted.

☐ You can use the browning dish for fillets or fish patties. Preheat, add butter or oil and brown on one side for best results.

☐ To remove seafood odors from the oven, combine 1 cup water with lemon juice and cloves in a small bowl. Boil in the microwave oven several minutes.

Using the Defrosting Guide

1. Frozen fish may be thawed in original wrapper. First discard any aluminum foil, metal rings, or wire twist ties.
2. Place fish on microproof dish. Remove wrapping when fish begins to thaw.
3. One pound of fish takes 5 to 6 minutes to nearly thaw on 30 (defrost).
4. To prevent the outer edges from drying out or beginning to cook, it is best to remove fish from oven before it has completely thawed.
5. Finish defrosting under cold running water, separating fillets.

DEFROSTING GUIDE — SEAFOOD

Food	Amount	Cook Control Setting	Time (in minutes)	Standing Time (in minutes)	Special Notes
Fish Fillets	1 lb. 2 lbs.	30 (defrost) 30 (defrost)	4 - 6 5 - 7	5 5	Defrost in package on dish. Carefully separate fillets under cold water. Turn once.
Fish steaks	1 lb.	30 (defrost)	4 - 6	5	Defrost in package on dish. Carefully separate steaks under cold running water.
Whole fish	8 - 10 oz. 1½ - 2 lbs.	30 (defrost) 30 (defrost)	4 - 6 5 - 7	5 5	Shallow dish; shape of fish determines size. Should be icy when removed. Finish at room temperature. Cover head with aluminum foil. Turn once.
Lobster tails	8 oz. package	30 (defrost)	5 - 7	5	Remove from package to baking dish.
Crab legs	8 - 10 oz.	30 (defrost)	5 - 7	5	Glass baking dish. Break apart and turn once.
Crabmeat	6 oz.	30 (defrost)	4 - 5	5	Defrost in package on dish. Break apart. Turn once.
Shrimp	1 lb.	30 (defrost)	3 - 4	5	Remove from package to dish. Spread loosely in baking dish and rearrange during thawing as necessary.
Scallops	1 lb.	30 (defrost)	8 - 10	5	Defrost in package if in block; spread out on baking dish if in pieces. Turn over and rearrange during thawing as necessary.
Oysters	12 oz.	30 (defrost)	3 - 4	5	Remove from package to dish. Turn over and rearrange during thawing as necessary.

Using the Cooking Guide

1. Defrost seafood fully; then cook.
2. Remove original wrapping. Rinse under cold running water.
3. Place seafood in microproof baking dish with thick edges of fillets and steaks and thick ends of shellfish toward the outer edge of the dish.
4. Cover dish with plastic wrap or waxed paper.
5. Test often during the cooking period to avoid overcooking.
6. Method and time are the same for seafood with or without the shell.

COOKING/DEFROSTING GUIDE — CONVENIENCE SEAFOOD

Food	Amount	Cook Control Setting	Time (in minutes)	Special Notes
Shrimp croquettes	12 oz. package	80 (reheat)	6 - 8	Pierce sauce pouch, place on serving plate with croquettes. Cover, turn halfway through cooking time.
Fish sticks, frozen	4 oz. 8 oz.	80 (reheat) 80 (reheat)	2 - 3 3½ - 4½	Will not crisp. Cook on serving plate.
Tuna casserole, frozen	11 oz. package	HI (max. power)	4 - 6	Remove from package to 1-quart casserole. Stir once during cooking and before serving.
Shrimp or crab newburg, frozen pouch	6½ oz.	HI (max. power)	4 - 6	Place pouch on plate. Pierce pouch. Flex pouch to mix halfway through cooking time. Stir before serving.

COOKING GUIDE — SEAFOOD AND FISH

Food	Cook Control Setting	Time (in Minutes)	or	Temperature Probe Setting	Standing Time (in minutes)	Special Notes
Fish fillets, 1 lb. ½ inch thick,	HI (max. power)	4 - 5	or	140°	4 - 5	12 × 7-inch dish, covered.
2 lbs.	HI (max. power)	7 - 8	or	140°	4 - 5	
Fish steaks, 1 inch thick, 1 lb.	HI (max. power)	5 - 6	or	140°	5 - 6	12 × 7-inch dish, covered.
Whole fish 8 - 10 oz.	HI (max. power)	3½ - 4	or	170°	3 - 4	Appropriate shallow dish.
1½ - 2 lbs.	HI (max. power)	5 - 7	or	170°	5	
Crab legs 8 - 10 oz.	HI (max. power)	3 - 4			5	Appropriate shallow dish, covered. Turn once.
16 - 20 oz.	HI (max. power)	5 - 6			5	
Shrimp, scallops 8 oz.	70 (roast)	3 - 4				Appropriate shallow dish, covered. Rearrange halfway.
1 lb.	70 (roast)	5 - 7				
Snails, clams, oysters, 12 oz.	70 (roast)	3 - 4				Shallow dish, covered. Rearrange halfway.
Lobster tails 1: 8 oz.	HI (max. power)	3 - 4			5	Shallow dish. Split shell to reduce curling.
2: 8 oz. each	HI (max. power)	5 - 6			5	
4: 8 oz. each	HI (max. power)	9 - 11			5	

Shrimp Chow Mein
Total Cooking Time: 20 to 24 minutes

1 medium onion, chopped
1 cup sliced celery
1 green pepper, cut in thin
    strips
2 tablespoons butter or
    margarine
1 can (16 ounces) bean
    sprouts, drained or
    1 pound fresh bean sprouts
½ cup sliced mushrooms
2 tablespoons chopped
    pimiento
8 to 10 ounces cooked
    cleaned shrimp
1 can (8 ounces) sliced water
    chestnuts, drained
3 tablespoons cornstarch
3 tablespoons soy sauce
1 cup water
2 teaspoons instant chicken
    bouillon

In 2-quart microproof casserole, place onion, celery, green pepper, and butter. Cook, covered, on HI (max. power) 9 to 10 minutes, or until tender. Add bean sprouts, mushrooms, pimiento, shrimp, and water chestnuts; set aside. In 4-cup glass measure, dissolve cornstarch into soy sauce. Add water and bouillon; mix well. Cook on HI (max. power) 6 to 7 minutes, or until mixture boils and thickens, stirring twice during cooking. Stir into shrimp mixture. Cook, covered, on HI (max. power) 5 to 7 minutes, or until hot. Stir once during cooking. Serve with hot cooked rice or Chinese noodles.

5 to 6 servings

Stuffed Bass

Total Cooking Time: 12 to 19½ minutes

Wash fish in cold water, pat dry, set aside. Place butter and onion in 1½-quart glass bowl. Cook on HI (max. power) 2 minutes, or until onion is transparent. Add all other ingredients except brown sauce and water. Mix well. Stuff fish with mixture. Place on oval microproof platter or 12×7×2-inch glass baking dish. Mix brown sauce and water, brush on fish. Shield head and tail with aluminum foil. Insert probe in meatiest part of fish, parallel with spine and in area close to probe receptacle. Do not let foil touch probe or wall of oven. Cover dish tightly with plastic wrap, but wrap loosely around probe to vent. Cook on HI (max. power) at 170°. Let stand 5 minutes before serving.

4 to 6 servings

Other whole fish of the same size may be substituted for bass, such as red snapper, lake trout, salmon, or whitefish. Whole stuffed fish may also be cooked by time (5 to 7 minutes per pound) on HI (max. power).

---

1 whole bass (2 to 2½ pounds), cleaned
2 tablespoons butter or margarine
¼ cup chopped onion
½ cup chopped mushrooms
¾ cup fine dry bread crumbs
2 tablespoons minced fresh parsley
1 egg, beaten
1 tablespoon lemon juice
1 teaspoon salt
⅛ teaspoon pepper
1 tablespoon bottled brown sauce
1 tablespoon water

Stuffed Flounder with Mushroom-Sherry Sauce

Total Cooking Time: 11¾ to 12¾ minutes

Place green onion, ¼ cup butter and chopped parsley in 2-quart microproof casserole. Cook on HI (max. power) 3 minutes, or until onion is transparent. Remove from oven. Drain mushrooms, reserving liquid. Drain crabmeat and shred with fork, picking out any cartilage. Add mushrooms, crabmeat, cracker crumbs, salt, and pepper to cooked onion and parsley, mixing well. Spread crabmeat stuffing over each flounder fillet. Roll fish and place, seam side down, in a 12×8-inch microproof baking dish. Set aside.

Place 2 tablespoons butter in 4-cup glass measure. Cook on HI (max. power) 45 seconds, or until melted. Stir in flour and salt. Add enough milk to mushroom liquid to make 1 cup. Combine liquid with sherry. Gradually stir milk-mushroom-sherry liquid into flour mixture, stirring briskly. Pour sauce over flounder. Cook on HI (max. power) 7 to 8 minutes. Sprinkle paprika and parsley over fish. Cook on HI (max. power) 1 minute. Serve immediately.

6 servings

¼ cup chopped green onion
¼ cup butter or margarine
2 tablespoons fresh chopped parsley
1 can (4 ounces) mushroom pieces
1 can (6½ ounces) crabmeat
½ cup cracker crumbs
½ teaspoon salt
¼ teaspoon pepper
6 small, thin fresh flounder fillets, or any white fish fillets (2 pounds)
2 tablespoons butter or margarine
2 tablespoons all-purpose flour
¼ teaspoon salt
Milk
⅓ cup dry sherry
½ teaspoon paprika
1 teaspoon fresh chopped parsley

Fillet of Fish Amandine

Total Cooking Time: 10 minutes

In 8-inch microproof baking dish place almonds and butter. Cook, uncovered, on HI (max. power) 5 minutes, or until almonds and butter are golden brown. Remove almonds and set aside. Place fish in dish with butter, turning to coat both sides. Sprinkle with salt, dill, pepper, parsley, and lemon juice. Roll fillets and leave in dish. Cover with waxed paper and cook on HI (max. power) 4 minutes. Uncover, sprinkle almonds on fish. Cook, covered, on HI (max. power) 1 minute, or until fish flakes with a fork. Let stand 4 minutes before serving. Garnish with lemon wedges, sprigs of parsley, and sprinkle with paprika.

½ cup slivered almonds
½ cup butter or margarine
1 pound fish fillets
½ teaspoon salt
¼ teaspoon dill weed
⅛ teaspoon pepper
1 teaspoon chopped fresh parsley
1 tablespoon lemon juice

2 to 3 servings

Fish Fillets with Mushrooms

Total Cooking Time: 5 minutes

Arrange fish fillets in 12×7×2-inch microproof baking dish with the thick edges toward the outside of dish. Dot with butter. Stir lemon juice into wine and sprinkle with remaining ingredients over top. Cover with waxed paper, cook on HI (max. power) 5 minutes. Let stand, covered, 5 minutes.

1 pound fish fillets
2 tablespoons butter or margarine
½ teaspoon lemon juice
2 tablespoons dry white wine
2 green onions, thinly sliced
½ cup sliced mushrooms
1 tomato, peeled and cubed
½ teaspoon salt

3 to 4 servings

This recipe may be cut to two servings by using ½ pound fish fillets (2 pieces), 1 small tomato, and half all the other ingredients. Cut cooking time to 2½ to 3 minutes.

Grilled Swordfish Steaks

Total Cooking Time: 6 to 7 minutes

Preheat 9-inch browning dish on HI (max. power) for 5 minutes. Brush swordfish steaks on one side only with oil. Sprinkle with lemon pepper and paprika. Place seasoned side down on preheated dish. Cook, covered, 1 to 2 minutes, or just until swordfish flakes. Turn over, cover, and let stand 2 minutes. Turn over and serve immediately.

2 swordfish steaks (8 ounces each)
1 tablespoon vegetable oil
Lemon pepper
Paprika

2 servings

← *Fillet of Fish Amandine*

Shrimp Creole

Total Cooking Time: 14 to 15 minutes

4   green onions, thinly sliced
¼   cup chopped celery
½   cup chopped green pepper
2   tablespoons butter or
      margarine
1   clove garlic, minced
1   can (16 ounces) whole
      tomatoes, drained and
      chopped
1   can (6 ounces) tomato paste
1   teaspoon salt
2   teaspoons dried parsley
      flakes
¼   teaspoon cayenne pepper
1   package (10 ounces) frozen
      cooked shrimp, thawed

In 2-quart microproof casserole, combine green onions, celery, green pepper, butter, and garlic. Cook, covered, on HI (max. power) 3 minutes, or until green onions are transparent. Stir in remaining ingredients. Cook, covered, on 80 (reheat) 5 minutes. Stir. Cook, covered, on 80 (reheat) 6 to 7 minutes, or until hot. Let stand, covered, 5 minutes before serving over hot cooked rice.

4 to 6 servings

Alternate method: The temperature probe may be used. Cook covered with plastic wrap on 80 (reheat) set at 150°.

Seafood Thermidor

Total Cooking Time: 15 to 18 minutes

1   pound fresh or frozen cod
      fillets
1   small onion, thinly sliced
1   teaspoon instant chicken
      bouillon
1   tablespoon lemon juice
2   teaspoons dill weed
1   cup water
1   can (10½ ounces) condensed
      cream of shrimp soup
3   tablespoons all-purpose
      flour
½   cup milk
½   cup shredded Swiss cheese
2   tablespoons chopped fresh
      parsley
1   tablespoon butter or
      margarine
½   cup bread crumbs
2   tablespoons grated
      Parmesan cheese
½   teaspoon paprika
2   parsley sprigs

Thaw fish, if frozen, according to chart on page 107. Cut into ¾-inch cubes. In 1½-quart microproof casserole, place onion, bouillon, lemon juice, dill weed, and water. Cook, covered, on HI (max. power) 2½ minutes, or until boiling. Add fish, cook, uncovered, on HI (max. power) 2 minutes, or until opaque. Remove fish with slotted spoon and set aside. Discard poaching mixture. In same casserole, blend soup and flour, gradually add milk. Cook, uncovered, on HI (max. power) 4 minutes, or until thickened and bubbly. Stir three times during cooking. Stir in Swiss cheese and parsley, and continue stirring until cheese is melted. Carefully place fish in sauce. In a 1-cup measure, melt butter on HI (max. power) 30 seconds, toss with bread crumbs, Parmesan cheese, and paprika. Sprinkle over casserole. Cook, uncovered, on HI (max. power) 2 to 3 minutes, or until edges are bubbly. Garnish with parsley sprigs.

4 servings

Shrimp Creole →

Tuna-Spinach Casserole

Total Cooking Time: 12¾ to 13¾ minutes

1 pound fresh spinach
1 can (7 ounces) tuna
1 can (4 ounces) sliced
   mushrooms
2 tablespoons lemon juice
2 tablespoons butter or
   margarine
1 tablespoon minced onion
2 tablespoons all-purpose
   flour
¼ teaspoon salt
⅛ teaspoon pepper
1 egg, lightly beaten
½ cup crumbled potato chips

Rinse spinach in cold water; drain well. Break in pieces, removing tough center stems. Place in 2-quart microproof casserole. Cook, covered, on HI (max. power) 3 to 4 minutes, or until spinach is limp. Drain well, set aside. Drain tuna, set aside. Drain mushrooms, pouring liquid into 1-cup measure. Set mushrooms aside. Add lemon juice and enough water to make 1 cup liquid. Place 2 tablespoons butter in 4-cup glass measure. Cook on HI (max. power) 45 seconds, or until melted. Add onion, flour, salt, and pepper, stirring well. Briskly stir in mushroom-lemon liquid. Cook, uncovered, on 60 (bake) 5 minutes, or until thick, stirring twice during cooking time. Add a small amount of sauce to egg, beat well, and return all to hot sauce. Stir mushrooms into sauce. Place well-drained spinach in 2½-quart microproof casserole. Flake tuna in small chunks over spinach. Pour sauce over top. Sprinkle with crumbled potato chips. Cook, uncovered, on HI (max. power) 4 minutes. Let stand 2 to 3 minutes before serving.

4 servings

Poached Salmon with Sour Cream Sauce

Total Cooking Time: 10 to 12 minutes

1½ cups hot water
⅓ cup dry white wine
2 peppercorns
1 lemon, thinly sliced
1 bay leaf
1 teaspoon instant minced
   onion
1 teaspoon salt
4 small salmon steaks or 2
   large steaks

Sauce:

½ cup dairy sour cream
1 tablespoon minced parsley
1 teaspoon lemon juice
½ teaspoon dill weed
   Pinch white pepper

In oval microproof baking dish pour water and wine, add peppercorns, lemon, bay leaf, onion, and salt. Cook on HI (max. power) 5 minutes, or until it reaches a full boil. Carefully place salmon steaks in hot liquid. Cook, covered with plastic wrap, on HI (max. power) 2 to 3 minutes, or until fish becomes opaque. Let stand 5 minutes to finish cooking. To prepare sauce, mix all ingredients in 2-cup glass measure. Cook on 50 (simmer) for 3 to 4 minutes, or until hot. Drain salmon and serve with heated sauce.

4 servings

Lemon Butter Sauce (page 153) is an excellent substitute for the Sour Cream Sauce.

To reduce calories omit the sauce and serve with lemon wedges and minced parsley.

This recipe is equally delicious with halibut, cod, swordfish, or red snapper.

Simple Salmon Loaf

Total Cooking Time: 25 to 30 minutes

Beat egg slightly and mix with remaining ingredients, until well blended. Pack salmon mixture firmly in greased 8×4×3-inch microproof loaf pan. Cover with waxed paper, cook on 70 (roast) 25 to 30 minutes, or until loaf is firm. Let stand, covered, 10 minutes before slicing.

6 to 8 servings

Alternate method: Before covering with waxed paper insert temperature probe into center of loaf. Cook on 70 (roast) at 150°F.

You can serve Simple Salmon Loaf with Lemon Butter Sauce (page 153) or Hot Lemony Dill Sauce (page 152).

This recipe may be cut in half by halving all ingredients except the egg. Form the loaf in an oval or round microproof dish. Cook, covered, on 70 (roast) 15 to 20 minutes.

1 egg
½ cup milk
¼ cup melted butter
3 slices soft bread, cubed
½ teaspoon salt
2 cans (16 ounces each) red salmon, drained, with bone and skin removed

Oysters Rockefeller

Total Cooking Time: 14 to 17 minutes

Carefully remove oysters from shells. Set aside. Select 36 shell halves; those that will sit level are best. Rinse well. Place, open side up, in two 12×7×2-inch microproof baking dishes. Set aside. Place spinach in 1½-quart microproof casserole. Cook, covered, on HI (max. power) 8 to 9 minutes. Drain well. Place between paper towels and squeeze dry. Mix spinach, butter, onion, parsley, salt, Worcestershire, pepper, and cream. Spoon half the spinach mixture into shells. Add one oyster to each shell. Top with remaining spinach mixture and generous sprinkling of Parmesan. Cover each baking dish with waxed paper. Place one dish on middle metal rack and one on bottom glass tray of oven. Cook on 70 (roast) 6 to 8 minutes, or until oysters are plump and edges curled. Reverse dishes after 3 minutes. Let stand 5 minutes before serving. Garnish with lemon wedges.

6 servings

This recipe can be halved. Place one dish on the bottom glass tray and cook at 70 (roast) for 5 minutes.

36 large oysters in the shell
1 package (10 ounces) frozen chopped spinach
2 tablespoons butter or margarine
1 tablespoon minced onion
3 tablespoons minced fresh parsley
½ teaspoon salt
1 tablespoon Worcestershire sauce
¼ teaspoon cayenne pepper
1 cup light cream
Parmesan cheese

Crab and Spinach Quiche

Total Cooking Time: 39 to 46 minutes

1 9-inch Homemade Pie Shell
1 package (6 ounces) frozen
   crabmeat
4 eggs
1 cup evaporated milk
1 teaspoon prepared mustard
⅛ teaspoon nutmeg
¾ teaspoon salt
2 tablespoons dry sherry
½ package (10 ounces) frozen
   chopped spinach, thawed
¾ cup shredded Swiss cheese

Cook pastry in glass pie plate according to directions on page 175. Set aside. In original package, thaw crabmeat on microproof plate on 30 (defrost) 3 to 4 minutes. Set aside. In large bowl, beat eggs. Add milk, mustard, nutmeg, salt, and sherry. Mix well. Drain spinach. Pick over crabmeat and remove any cartilage. Add spinach, cheese, and crabmeat to egg mixture. Stir well. Pour into prepared pastry shell. Cook on 60 (bake) for 30 to 35 minutes, or until nearly set in center. Rotate dish one-quarter turn at 10-minute intervals during cooking time. Let stand 5 minutes before serving.

6 servings

To thaw only the amount of spinach required, wrap one-half of the package with aluminum foil. Set on paper towel and thaw on 30 (defrost) for 3 to 4 minutes. Remove thawed portion from package. Return frozen portion to freezer.

Scallops Vermouth

Total Cooking Time: 13 minutes

¼ cup butter or margarine
1 tablespoon minced onion
2 tablespoons all-purpose
   flour
1 can (4 ounces) sliced
   mushrooms, drained
¼ cup dry vermouth
½ teaspoon salt
⅛ teaspoon pepper
1 pound bay scallops
1 bay leaf
2 teaspoons lemon juice
½ cup light cream
1 egg yolk
½ teaspoon hot pepper
   sauce (optional)
1 tablespoon chopped fresh
   parsley

Combine butter and onion in 2-quart microproof casserole. Cook, uncovered, on HI (max. power) 2 minutes. Stir in flour and blend well. Add mushrooms, wine, salt, pepper, scallops, bay leaf, and lemon juice. Stir carefully. Cook, covered, on HI (max. power) 6 minutes, or until scallops are tender. Remove bay leaf. Beat cream with egg yolk. Add some of the hot liquid carefully to egg and blend well. Stir egg mixture carefully into hot casserole. Add pepper sauce and stir well. Cook, covered, on 60 (bake) 5 minutes, stirring once during cooking. Sprinkle with parsley and serve.

4 servings

Eggs and cheese are great microwave partners; but they can stand by themselves, too. There's nothing quite like plain scrambled eggs or cheese fondue made in the microwave oven. From the simplest omelets to fancy quiches, the microwave oven can enliven an ordinary breakfast, Sunday brunch, or any meal. The recipes in this chapter are perfect for unexpected guests any time of day. Just remember to have on hand a carton of fresh eggs and some Cheddar or Swiss cheeses that keep well. Then, a little onion and seasonings are all you need to make a quick, easy, and delicious meal. As a special treat, we have included in this chapter a special recipe for making yogurt from scratch! One reminder: Do not hardboil eggs in the microwave oven. Pressure builds up inside the shell, which causes the egg to burst. Egg yolks should always be carefully pierced before cooking to prevent them from popping. Keep in mind that eggs and cheese are delicate ingredients; handle them with care and you will have delectable results.

Omelet Classique (page 120) is cooked and served in the same dish (above left). Just a flip makes your Sunny Side Up Eggs (page 120) become "Over Easy" if that's your preference (above). Refrigerated cheese can be quickly brought to room temperature at 60 (bake) for 1 minute (left).

Converting Your Recipes

The best advice for adapting recipes that use eggs and cheese as primary ingredients is "better to undercook than overcook." Cheese and eggs cook so quickly that a few seconds can make the difference between airy excellence and a rubbery disaster. You will be able to make countless variations on the recipes here, substituting vegetables and cooked meat, and adding your own spices and sauces. Conventional soufflé recipes do not adapt to microwave cooking. Microwave soufflé recipes require a special form of stabilization because they cook so quickly; therefore, evaporated milk is used for the cream sauce base. The tips below will guide you to microwave success with all your egg and cheese recipes:

- ☐ Undercook eggs slightly and allow standing time to complete cooking. Eggs become tough when overcooked. Always check doneness to avoid overcooking.
- ☐ Cover poaching or baking eggs to trap steam and ensure even cooking.
- ☐ Eggs are usually cooked at 60 (bake) or 70 (roast).
- ☐ If you want a soft yolk, remove the egg from oven before whites are completely cooked. A brief standing time allows whites to set without overcooking yolks.
- ☐ Add $1/8$ to $1/4$ teaspoon vinegar to the water when poaching eggs to help the white coagulate.
- ☐ Cook bacon and egg combinations on HI (max. power), since most of the microwaves are attracted to the bacon because of its high fat content.
- ☐ Omelets and scrambled eggs should be stirred at least once during cooking. Fondues and sauces profit from occasional stirring during the cooking time.
- ☐ Cheese melts quickly and makes an attractive topping for casseroles and sandwiches.
- ☐ Cook cheese on 70 (roast) or lower for short periods of time to avoid separation and toughening.

Using the Cooking Guides

1. Eggs should be at refrigerator temperature.
2. Eggs will continue to cook for 1 or 2 minutes after removal from oven, so remove just before done.
3. *To scramble:* Break eggs into a microproof bowl or 4-cup glass measure. Add milk or cream. Beat with a fork. Add butter. Cover with waxed paper. Cook at 60 (bake) for time indicated in chart. Stir at least once during cooking from the outside to the center. Let stand 1 minute before serving.
4. *To poach:* Bring water to a boil with a pinch of salt and up to $1/4$ teaspoon vinegar at HI (max. power). Break egg carefully into hot water. Pierce egg lightly with toothpick. Cover with waxed paper. Cook at 50 (simmer) for time required in chart. Let stand, covered, 1 minute before serving.

COOKING GUIDE — SCRAMBLED EGGS

Number of Eggs	Liquid (Milk or Cream)	Butter	Minutes to Cook
1	1 tablespoon	1 teaspoon	1 to 1½
2	2 tablespoons	2 teaspoons	2 to 2½
4	3 tablespoons	3 teaspoons	4½ to 5½
6	4 tablespoons	4 teaspoons	7 to 8

COOKING GUIDE — POACHED EGGS

Number of Eggs	Water	Container	Minutes to Boil Water	Minutes to Cook
1	¼ cup	6-ounce microproof custard cup	1½ to 2	1
2	¼ cup	6-ounce microproof custard cups	2	1½ to 2
3	¼ cup	6-ounce microproof custard cups	2 to 2½	2 to 2½
4	1 cup	1-quart microproof dish	2½ to 3	2½ to 3

COOKING GUIDE — CONVENIENCE EGGS AND CHEESE

Food	Amount	Cook Control Setting	Time (in minutes)	Special Notes
Omelet, frozen	10 oz.	80 (reheat)	4 - 5	Use microproof plate.
Egg substitute	8 oz.	50 (simmer)	4 - 4½	Turn carton over after 1 minute. Open carton after 1½ minutes. Stir every 30 seconds until smooth.
Souffles: Corn, frozen	12 oz.	HI (max. power)	10 - 12	Use 1½-quart casserole, covered. Rotate casserole twice.
Cheese, frozen	12 oz.	HI (max. power)	11 - 13	Use 1½-quart casserole, covered. Rotate casserole twice.
Spinach, frozen	12 oz.	HI (max. power)	12 - 15	Use 1½-quart casserole, covered. Rotate casserole twice.
Welsh rabbit, frozen	10 oz.	70 (roast)	6 - 7	Use 1½-quart casserole, covered. Stir during cooking time.

Quiche Lorraine
Total Cooking Time: 26 to 30 minutes

1 baked 9-inch Homemade Pie
  Shell (page 175) or Low
  Calorie Rice Crust (page 136)
6 slices bacon
3 green onions, thinly
  sliced
2 cups grated Swiss cheese
1 can (13 ounces) evaporated
  milk
¼ teaspoon salt
¼ teaspoon nutmeg
  Dash cayenne pepper
1 teaspoon prepared mustard
4 eggs, beaten

Prepare baked pie shell. If pie shell is purchased, transfer it to a glass pie plate for baking. Cook crisp bacon according to chart on page 71. Crumble into small pieces. Reserve about 1 tablespoon each of bacon and onions for topping. Spread remaining bacon and onions with cheese evenly in pie shell. In 2-cup measure heat milk on HI (max. power) 3 minutes, or until it reaches boiling point. Mix salt, nutmeg, pepper, and mustard into beaten eggs. Gradually pour hot milk into egg mixture while continuing to mix. Pour carefully into pie shell. Sprinkle reserved bacon and onions over top. Cook on 70 (roast) 12 to 14 minutes, or until center appears barely set. Let stand uncovered on bread board or heat-proof counter top covered with foil 10 minutes before cutting.

6 servings

Omelet Classique
Total Cooking Time: 5 to 5½ minutes

1 tablespoon butter or
  margarine
4 eggs
4 tablespoons water
½ teaspoon salt
⅛ teaspoon pepper

In 9-inch microproof pie plate, cook butter on HI (max. power) 30 seconds, or until melted. Beat remaining ingredients lightly with a fork. Pour into pie plate. Cover with waxed paper, cook on 70 (roast) 3 minutes. Stir lightly. Cook, covered, on 60 (bake) 1½ to 2 minutes, or until almost set in center. Let stand, covered, 1 to 2 minutes before serving. Fold in half and serve.

2 servings

Before folding omelet, top with crumbled cooked bacon, grated Cheddar cheese, chopped cooked ham, or chopped tomato.

Sunny-Side-Up Eggs
Total Cooking Time: 2½ to 3 minutes

1 tablespoon butter or
  margarine
2 eggs
  Salt
  Pepper

Preheat 9-inch browning dish on HI (max. power) 2 minutes. Add butter and allow to melt. Tip dish to coat surface. Break eggs into dish and pierce yolks. Sprinkle lightly with dash of salt and pepper. Cover with glass lid; cook on HI (max. power) 30 to 60 seconds, according to your preference in yolk firmness. Let stand for 1 minute before serving.

1 to 2 servings

Quiche Lorraine →

Homemade Yogurt

Total Cooking Time: 12 minutes*

1⅓ cups non-fat dry milk
1 cup whole or 2% milk
1 can (5⅓-ounces)
   evaporated milk
⅓ cup plain yogurt

In 4-cup glass measure combine dry milk and enough water to make 2 cups milk. Stir to dissolve dry milk. Pour into 2-quart glass casserole and stir in whole milk. Insert temperature probe in center of mixture. Cook on HI (max. power) with probe set at 190°. (If you do not use probe, cook for 8 minutes.) Remove from oven, stir in evaporated milk. Cool mixture to 115°.

Blend a small amount of milk mixture into yogurt, then stir yogurt into milk. Insert probe into center of mixture. Cover with plastic wrap. Cook on 30 (defrost) at 115°. If possible, leave yogurt in oven during 3 hours setting time. Check every hour to insure that temperature of yogurt stays in 110° to 115° range. By setting "cook control" at 30 (defrost) and "temperature control" at 115°, the display window will record the temperature. The oven will automatically continue to bring temperature back up to 115° when you reset it every hour. (If you cannot leave the mixture in the oven, place it in a warm place out of drafts and check temperature with regular thermometer periodically, not allowing the temperature to go below 110°. When the temperature goes below 110°, return the yogurt to microwave oven, insert probe set at 115° at 30 (defrost). Continue procedure until 3 hours setting time has been reached.) After 3 hours setting time, stir until smooth and chill, covered, in refrigerator. Yogurt may be stored in small containers, as is, or after flavoring.

3 cups

Timing is difficult to determine accurately because it takes very little cooking time if left in the oven to set. It will require closer attention if removed from the cozy microwave! If, after 3 hours, the yogurt does not seem as set as you would like, allow a little more time. Suggested flavorings:

Fruit jam yogurt: Add 1 to 2 tablespoons of your favorite jam to 1 cup yogurt.
Fresh fruit yogurt: Add ¼ to ½ cup crushed or finely chopped fruit to 1 cup yogurt. Sweeten as necessary.
Honey yogurt: Add 1 tablespoon honey to 1 cup yogurt.
Dried fruit yogurt: Add ¼ to ½ cup chopped prunes or apricots to 1 cup yogurt.
Orange yogurt: Add 1 tablespoon orange juice concentrate to 1 cup yogurt.
Vegetable yogurt: Add chopped fresh radishes, cucumbers, celery, carrot, tomatoes, green onions (in any combination) to 1 cup yogurt.

Eggs in Nests

Total Cooking Time: 5 to 5½ minutes

Slice tops from tomatoes. Scoop out pulp and turn shells upside down on paper towels to drain. Discard seeds, chop pulp, and mix with parsley. Combine butter and onion in small microproof mixing bowl. Cover with paper towel and cook on HI (max. power) about 4 minutes. Add parsley-tomato pulp mixture, stirring well. Divide into tomato shells. Break 1 egg into each tomato shell, pierce yolk carefully with toothpick. Season lightly with salt and pepper. Place tomatoes in 8-inch microproof baking dish. Cover with waxed paper and cook on 60 (bake) 1 to 1½ minutes, or until eggs are set to desired degree of doneness.

8 small, firm, ripe tomatoes
¼ cup chopped parsley
¼ cup butter or margarine
1 large onion, finely chopped
8 eggs
   Salt and pepper

8 servings

Eggs Benedict

Total Cooking Time: 11 to 13 minutes

Prepare Hollandaise Sauce according to recipe on page 154. Cover with piece of waxed paper and set aside. Place each muffin half on a paper towel-lined microproof plate and top each with 1 slice ham. Cook, uncovered, two at a time, on 60 (bake) 2 to 2½ minutes, or until ham is hot. Top each with poached egg prepared as instructed on page 119. Cover with Hollandaise Sauce and serve immediately.

¾ cup Hollandaise Sauce
2 English muffins, split and
   toasted
4 slices boiled ham, ¼
   inch thick
4 poached eggs

4 servings

Fiesta Scramble

Total Cooking Time: 9¼ to 10¼ minutes

In 10-inch microproof pie plate melt butter on HI (max. power) 45 seconds. Tilt dish to coat. Spread tomatoes, chilies, and chives evenly on pie plate. Cook on HI (max. power) 1½ minutes, or until vegetables are softened. Beat eggs with milk, garlic powder, salt, and pepper. Add to tomato mixture and cook, uncovered, on 70 (roast) about 6 minutes or until nearly set, stirring frequently from center to outside. Eggs should still be slightly moist. Sprinkle cheese over top, cook on 70 (roast) 1 to 2 minutes, or until cheese is melted. Sprinkle with parsley and serve.

2 tablespoons butter or
   margarine
2 small tomatoes, peeled,
   seeded, and chopped
1 can (4 ounces) diced green
   chilies
1 tablespoon minced chives
6 eggs
6 tablespoons milk
⅛ teaspoon garlic powder
¼ teaspoon salt
   Dash pepper
1 cup grated sharp Cheddar
   cheese
2 tablespoons minced fresh
   parsley

4 servings

Welsh Rabbit on Toast

Total Cooking Time: 13 minutes

4 teaspoons butter or
   margarine
4 cups shredded sharp
   Cheddar cheese
¾ teaspoon Worcestershire
   sauce
½ teaspoon salt
½ teaspoon paprika
¼ teaspoon dry mustard
¼ teaspoon cayenne pepper
2 eggs, lightly beaten
1 cup flat beer or ale, at
   room temperature
8 to 12 toasted French
   bread slices

In 2-quart microproof casserole, melt butter on HI (max. power) 1 minute. Add cheese, Worcestershire, salt, paprika, dry mustard, and cayenne; mix thoroughly. Cook, covered, on 50 (simmer) 6 minutes, stirring once during cooking time. Stir small amount of hot cheese mixture into the beaten eggs, then slowly add to hot mixture; stir briskly. Gradually stir in beer, blend well. Cook, covered, on 50 (simmer) 3 minutes. Stir well. Cook, covered, on 50 (simmer) 3 minutes longer. Remove from oven. Beat briskly with whisk to blend thoroughly. Serve over toasted and buttered French bread.

4 to 6 servings

For a hearty meal serve Welsh Rabbit with crisp bacon slices and garnished with tomatoes.

Puffy Cheddar Omelet

Total Cooking Time: 7½ to 9½ minutes

4 eggs, separated
⅓ cup mayonnaise
2 tablespoons water
1 tablespoon butter or
   margarine
½ cup grated Cheddar
   cheese
1 tablespoon minced
   fresh parsley

In large mixing bowl, beat egg whites with electric mixer until soft peaks form. In small mixing bowl beat egg yolks with mayonnaise and water. Gently fold yolks into whites. In 9-inch microproof pie plate melt butter on HI (max. power) 30 seconds. Tilt dish to coat evenly. Pour egg mixture into pie plate. Cook on 60 (bake) 6 or 8 minutes. Rotate dish if eggs appear to be rising unevenly. When eggs are set but still moist, sprinkle with cheese. Cook on 60 (bake) for 1 minute, or until cheese is melted. Fold omelet in half and slide onto serving plate. Sprinkle with parsley.

2 servings

Shirred Eggs

Total Cooking Time: 2½ to 3 minutes

1 teaspoon butter or
   margarine
2 eggs
1 tablespoon cream
   Salt and pepper

Place butter in microproof ramekin or small cereal bowl. Cook on 70 (roast) 30 seconds to melt. Break eggs carefully into ramekin. Pierce yolks carefully with toothpick. Add cream. Cover tightly with plastic wrap and cook on 60 (bake) 2 to 2½ minutes. Remove and let stand 1 minute before serving. Season to taste.

1 serving

Welsh Rabbit on Toast →

Cheddar Cheese Soufflé
Total Cooking Time: 24 to 30 minutes

¼ cup all-purpose flour
¾ teaspoon salt
½ teaspoon dry mustard
⅛ teaspoon paprika
⅛ teaspoon white pepper
1 can (13-ounces)
  evaporated milk,
  undiluted
2 cups grated sharp Cheddar
  cheese
6 eggs, separated
1 teaspoon cream of tartar

In 4-cup glass measure blend flour, salt, mustard, paprika, and pepper. Add evaporated milk and stir. Cook on HI (max. power) 4 to 5 minutes, or until thickened, stirring after 2 minutes and then every 30 seconds. Stir in cheese and continue stirring until cheese is melted. Remove from oven. In large mixing bowl beat egg whites with cream of tartar until stiff but not dry. Set aside. In small mixing bowl beat yolks until thick. Slowly pour warm cheese mixture over egg yolks, stirring until well combined. Spoon mixture over egg whites and fold gently to blend. Turn into ungreased 2-quart microproof soufflé dish. Cook on 30 (defrost) for 20 to 25 minutes, or until top is dry. Rotate dish if soufflé is rising unevenly. Serve immediately.

8 servings

Because microwave soufflés do not form a crust, they rise higher than conventional soufflé recipes and require a larger dish. When done, the soufflé will be dry on top but will have a creamy meringue center, which is nice as the sauce for the soufflé. Do not try to adapt conventional soufflés to microwave cooking.

Swiss Cheese Fondue
Total Cooking Time: 10 to 11 minutes

3 tablespoons all-purpose
  flour
¼ teaspoon salt
⅛ teaspoon white pepper
½ teaspoon garlic powder
1 cup milk
1 pound Swiss cheese,
  shredded
1 tablespoon butter or
  margarine
½ cup dry white wine
  Dash nutmeg

In a 1½-quart glass casserole, combine flour, seasonings, and milk. Beat with wire whisk until smooth. Stir in cheese, add butter. Cook, covered, on 70 (roast) 5 minutes. Stir well, cook, covered, on 70 (roast) 5 to 6 minutes, or until thickened and smooth. The probe may be used on 70 (roast) set at 180°. Stir in wine and nutmeg. Serve warm from fondue pot or chafing dish.

3 cups

This is a nifty hors d'oeuvre for a cold winter's night as well as a great main dish any time. Serve with crusty French, Italian, rye, whole wheat, or herb bread cut into 1 to 1½-inch cubes. Or try bread sticks and pretzels. Fondue may be made ahead, refrigerated, and reheated. To reheat, cook, covered, on 70 (roast) about 8 minutes, or until warm. Stir well before serving.

The microwave oven provides no significant saving of time when cooking pasta and rice. It takes just as long to rehydrate these products in the microwave oven as it does conventionally. But the convenience of being able to cook and serve in the same dish, and to eliminate scorching and food stuck to pans makes it well worthwhile. Once the pasta is prepared and added to the rest of the ingredients according to the recipe, the casserole cooks in speedy microwave time. Another great advantage the microwave oven offers is that you can reheat pasta, rice, and cereal without adding water or having to stir. No worry about soggy noodles or starchy rice. And they taste as good reheated as when freshly cooked!

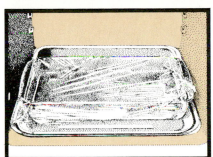

The microwave works wonders with pasta: simply top precooked macaroni or rotini with sauce, tomato slices, and cheese for a dandy lunch (top left). Cook rice in boilable bags on a plate with the bag slit so steam can escape (top right). Spaghetti is cooked in a glass baking dish (above left). Hot cereal is now easy to prepare and serve right in the same dish (above right).

Converting Your Recipes

You will find that your conventional rice or noodle-based casseroles can be easily adjusted to microwave cooking. When you find a similar recipe here, adapt your ingredients to the microwave method, but follow only about three-quarters of the recommended microwave cooking times. Then check, observe, and extend the cooking time at 1-minute intervals until done. Make a note of the final cooking time for a repeat of the dish. By "trial" and trying to avoid "error," you'll soon be able to add to your collection of pasta and rice dishes. These tips will help:

☐ Casseroles cooked in the microwave oven usually need less liquid. Because of their shorter cooking time, there is less evaporation.

☐ Casseroles with cream and cheese sauces or less tender meats that require slow cooking do best on low settings.

☐ It is important to use a large microproof container when cooking pasta or rice to prevent water from boiling over.

☐ Thin noodles cook faster and more evenly than large noodles.

☐ Casseroles may require occasional stirring to distribute heat.

☐ Cook the ingredients of a casserole and stir before adding topping, such as cheese or bread crumbs.

☐ Cooked pasta or rice to be used in a casserole should be slightly firmer than if it is to be eaten at once. Simply cook a bit less.

☐ Quick-cooking rice may be substituted in converting from conventional recipes that call for uncooked rice, in order to make sure the rice will cook in the same short time as the rest of the ingredients. Otherwise precook regular rice to a firm stage and add to the casserole.

☐ To reheat pasta, rice, and cereals in the microwave without drying out, cover tightly with plastic wrap. Set at 80 (reheat) for just a few minutes, depending upon amount.

Using The Cooking Guides

1. For pasta, combine water with 1 tablespoon salad oil and 1 to 2 teaspoons salt in microproof container. Bring water to a boil on HI (max. power). Stir. Cover. Cook at 50 (simmer) until done. Drain in colander, rinse in warm water. Serve.

2. For rice, add salt and margarine to water according to package directions. Bring water to full boil on HI (max. power). Stir in rice. Cover tightly. Cook on 50 (simmer) for time provided in chart. Let stand, covered, 5 minutes before serving.

3. For quick-cooking cereal, follow chart and package recommendations. Stir after removing from oven. Let stand about 1 minute before serving

COOKING GUIDE — PASTA

Food	Amount Uncooked (2 oz. = 1 cup)	Hot Tap Water	Time to Boil (in minutes) HI (max. power)	Cook Control Setting	Time (in minutes)	Special Notes
Spaghetti or linguine	2 oz.	2½ cups	5 - 6	50 (simmer)	5 - 6	Use 13×9×2-inch baking dish. Stir once.
	4 oz.	4 cups	8 - 10	50 (simmer)	6 - 8	
	7 oz.	6 cups	12 - 14	50 (simmer)	8 - 10	
Macaroni	4 oz.	3 cups	6 - 8	50 (simmer)	10 - 12	Use 3-quart casserole.
Egg noodles, fine	2 oz.	2 cups	4 - 6	50 (simmer)	5 - 6	Use 3-quart casserole.
Egg noodles, narrow	4 oz.	3 cups	6 - 8	50 (simmer)	8 - 10	
Egg noodles, wide	8 oz.	6 cups	12 - 14	50 (simmer)	12 - 14	
Lasagna noodles	4 oz.	4 cups	8 - 10	50 (simmer)	12 - 14	Use 13×9×2-inch baking dish.
	8 oz.	6 cups	12 - 14	50 (simmer)	14 - 15	
Spinach noodles	4 oz.	4 cups	8 - 10	50 (simmer)	9 - 11	Use 13×9×2-inch baking dish.

COOKING GUIDE — RICE

Food	Amount Uncooked	Water	Minutes to Full Boil HI (max. power)	Cook Control Setting	Time (in minutes)	Standing Time (in minutes)	Special Notes
Short-grain	1 cup	2 cups	4 - 5	50 (simmer)	13 - 15	5	2-quart casserole
Long-grain	1 cup	2 cups	4 - 5	50 (simmer)	15 - 17	5	2-quart casserole
Wild rice	1 cup	3 cups	6 - 7	50 (simmer)	35 - 40	5	3-quart casserole
Brown rice	1 cup	3 cups	6 - 7	50 (simmer)	40	5	3-quart casserole
Quick-cooking	1 cup	1 cup	3 - 4	HI (max. power)	0	5	1-quart casserole

COOKING/DEFROSTING GUIDE — CONVENIENCE RICE AND PASTA

Food	Amount	Cook Control Setting	Time (in minutes)	Special Notes
Rice, cooked refrigerated	1 cup	80 (reheat)	1½ - 2	Use covered bowl. Let stand 2 minutes, stir.
Cooked, frozen	1 cup	80 (reheat)	2 - 3	
	2 cups	80 (reheat)	3 - 4	
Pouch, frozen	11 oz.	80 (reheat)	6 - 7	Slit pouch.
Fried rice, frozen	10 oz.	HI (max. power)	5 - 6	Use covered casserole. Stir twice. Let stand 5 minutes.
Spanish rice, canned	12 oz.	HI (max. power)	4 - 5	Use covered casserole. Stir twice. Let stand 3 minutes.
Lasagna, frozen	21 oz.	70 (roast)	19 - 20	Use covered casserole. Let stand, covered, 5 minutes.
Macaroni and beef, frozen	11 oz. package	HI (max. power)	7 - 9	Use covered casserole. Stir twice.
Macaroni and cheese, frozen	10 oz.	HI (max. power)	7 - 9	Use covered casserole. Stir twice.
Spaghetti and meatballs, frozen	14 oz.	HI (max. power)	8 - 10	Use covered casserole. Stir twice.

COOKING GUIDE — CEREAL

Food	Servings	Amount Uncooked	Salt	Hot Tap Water	Setting	Minutes To Cook	Special Notes
Quick grits	1	3 Tb.	dash	¾ cup	HI (max. power)	3 - 4	10-oz. bowl
	2	⅓ cup	¼ tsp.	1⅓ cups	HI (max. power)	6 - 7	1½-qt. bowl
	4	⅔ cup	¾ tsp.	2⅔ cups	HI (max. power)	8 - 9	2-qt. bowl
Oatmeal, quick	1	⅓ cup	⅛ tsp.	¾ cup	HI (max. power)	1 - 2	16-oz. bowl
	2	⅔ cup	¼ tsp.	1½ cups	HI (max. power)	2 - 3	1½-qt. bowl
	4	1⅓ cups	½ tsp.	3 cups	HI (max. power)	5 - 6	2-qt. bowl
Cream of wheat	1	2½ Tb.	dash	1 cup	HI (max. power)	3 - 4	1-qt. bowl
	2	⅓ cup	⅛ tsp.	1¾ cups	HI (max. power)	5 - 6	2-qt. bowl
	4	⅔ cup	¼ tsp.	3½ cups	HI (max. power)	7 - 8	3-qt. bowl

Chicken Noodle au Gratin
Total Cooking Time: 13 to 15 minutes

1½ cups uncooked broken thin
      egg noodles
  2 to 3 cups cubed cooked
      chicken or turkey
  1 cup chicken stock
½ cup milk
½ teaspoon salt
⅛ teaspoon pepper
  1 cup shredded Cheddar
      cheese
¼ cup sliced stuffed green
      olives

In 2-quart microproof casserole, combine noodles, chicken, chicken stock, milk, salt, and pepper. Stir lightly. Cook, covered, on 70 (roast) 8 to 10 minutes, or until noodles are tender, stirring once. Stir in cheese and olives. Cook, covered, on 20 (low) 5 minutes, or until cheese is melted.

4 to 6 servings

For 2 to 3 servings, cut ingredients in half and cook, covered, on 70 (roast) 6 to 8 minutes, or until noodles are tender, stirring once. Continue as directed for full recipe.

Spring Noodle Casserole
Total Cooking Time: 37½ to 43½ minutes

1½ cups uncooked spinach
      noodles
¼ cup butter or margarine
¼ cup all-purpose flour
  1 teaspoon salt
¼ teaspoon hot-pepper sauce
2¼ cups milk
  1 cup grated sharp Cheddar
      cheese
¼ cup grated Parmesan cheese
  3 hard-cooked eggs, peeled
      and halved

Cook spinach noodles according to chart on page 129. Drain and set aside. Place butter in 1½-quart microproof mixing bowl. Cook on HI (max. power) 60 seconds, or until melted. Stir in flour, salt, and hot-pepper sauce to make smooth paste. Cook on HI (max. power) 30 seconds. Set aside. Pour milk in 4-cup glass measure. Cook on HI (max. power) 2 minutes to warm. Gradually, and briskly, stir milk into flour mixture. Cook on HI (max. power) 4 to 5 minutes. Stir once during cooking time. Stir briskly to make smooth sauce. Add cheese and stir until melted. Put cooked noodles in 2-quart microproof casserole. Add cheese sauce and mix carefully. Cook, covered, on 60 (bake) 7 to 8 minutes, or until hot. Stir. Top with egg halves. Cook, covered, on 60 (bake) 3 minutes. Let stand, covered, 3 minutes before serving.

6 servings

Macaroni and Cheese

Total Cooking Time: 22½ to 25 minutes

Cook macaroni according to chart on page 129. Drain and set aside. In 4-cup glass measure melt butter on HI (max. power) for 45 seconds. Stir in flour, salt, Worcestershire, mustard, and pepper. Set aside. Pour milk in 2-cup glass measure and cook on HI (max. power) 1 minute, or until warm. Gradually stir milk into flour mixture. Cook on HI (max. power) 3 minutes, stirring once during cooking. Stir, cook on HI (max. power) 1 minute, or until smooth and thickening. Blend in 1½ cups of cheese. Stir until melted. In 1½-quart microproof casserole, combine sauce and cooked macaroni. Combine remaining cheese and cracker crumbs. Sprinkle over top of casserole. Cook on 60 (bake) 5 to 6 minutes, or until mixture is bubbling. Let stand, covered, 5 minutes before serving.

4 servings

1¼ cups uncooked macaroni
2 tablespoons butter or margarine
2 tablespoons all-purpose flour
¼ teaspoon salt
½ teaspoon Worcestershire sauce
½ teaspoon prepared mustard
⅛ teaspoon pepper
1 cup milk
2 cups shredded Cheddar cheese, divided
¼ cup cracker crumbs

Neapolitan Lasagna

Total Cooking Time: 46 to 53 minutes

Cook noodles according to chart on page 129. Drain and set aside, covered. Crumble beef into 2-quart glass mixing bowl. Cook on HI (max. power) 4 minutes. Stir halfway through cooking time. Pour off drippings. Combine meat with the tomato purée, mushrooms, onion, garlic, basil, oregano, thyme, salt, and pepper. Cook on HI (max. power) 6 to 8 minutes. Stir halfway through cooking time. Layer one-third of cooked noodles in 12 × 7 × 2-inch baking dish. Top with one-third of meat mixture and half of cottage cheese and mozzarella. Repeat layers, ending with noodles and meat sauce. Sprinkle generously with Parmesan cheese. Cover with waxed paper and cook on HI (max. power) 10 to 12 minutes, rotating dish one-quarter turn halfway through cooking time. Let stand, covered, 5 to 10 minutes before serving.

6 to 8 servings

5 ounces lasagna noodles, cooked
1 pound lean ground beef
1 can (16 ounces) tomato purée
¼ pound mushrooms, chopped
1 small onion, minced
1 clove garlic, minced
1 teaspoon basil
1 teaspoon oregano
½ teaspoon thyme
½ teaspoon salt
¼ teaspoon pepper
1½ cups cottage cheese, divided
10 ounces mozzarella cheese, sliced, divided
½ cup freshly grated Parmesan cheese

Spaghetti Bolognese

Total Cooking Time: 30 to 35 minutes

Crumble beef into 3-quart microproof casserole. Add onion and garlic. Cook on HI (max. power) 5 minutes. Stir to break up meat, drain off excess fat. Add remaining ingredients, except spaghetti. Cut tomatoes into small pieces with wooden spoon. Cook, covered, on 50 (simmer) 25 to 30 minutes, or until mixture is well blended and slightly thickened. Cover and let stand about 5 minutes. Serve over hot cooked spaghetti.

About 1½ quarts sauce
10 servings

- 1 pound lean ground beef
- ½ cup chopped onion
- 2 cloves garlic, minced
- 1 can (28 ounces) tomatoes
- 2 cans (6 ounces each) tomato paste
- 2 teaspoons salt
- 2 teaspoons oregano
- ¼ teaspoon basil
- ¼ teaspoon thyme
- ⅛ teaspoon pepper
  Cooked spaghetti (page 129)

Kentucky Cheddar Grits

Total Cooking Time: 21 to 26 minutes

In 3-quart microproof casserole, stir together water, grits, and salt. Cook on HI (max. power) 10 to 12 minutes, stirring halfway through cooking time. Add butter and cheese, stir well. Cook on HI (max. power) 1 to 2 minutes, or until cheese is melted. Stir well. Add to beaten eggs the Worcestershire sauce, garlic, and hot-pepper sauce. Stir into grits. Cook on 70 (roast) 10 to 12 minutes, or until almost set in center. Let stand 5 minutes before serving.

8 servings

- 4 cups water
- 1 cup uncooked quick grits
- 1 teaspoon salt
- ½ cup butter or margarine
- 1 cup grated sharp Cheddar cheese
- 2 eggs, beaten
- 1 tablespoon Worcestershire sauce
- ¼ teaspoon garlic powder
- ¼ teaspoon hot-pepper sauce

Spanish Rice

Total Cooking Time: 35 to 40 minutes

In 2-quart microproof casserole, combine all ingredients except rice. Cook, covered, on HI (max. power) 5 minutes, or until boiling. Stir in rice. Cook, covered, on 50 (simmer) 30 to 35 minutes, or until rice is tender. Let stand, covered, 5 minutes before serving.

6 to 8 servings

- 1½ cups water
- 1 can (16 ounces) tomatoes, chopped
- 1 can (6 ounces) tomato paste
- ¼ cup finely chopped onion
- 1 teaspoon sugar
- 1 teaspoon salt
- ¼ cup chopped celery
- ½ teaspoon oregano
- 1 clove garlic, minced
- ⅔ cup long-grain white rice

← *Spaghetti Bolognese*

Macaroni Supreme

Total Cooking Time: 1 hour 1 minute to
1 hour 7 minutes

2 cups uncooked elbow
    macaroni
1 pound lean ground beef
1 large onion, finely chopped
1 can (1 pound 12 ounces)
    Italian-style tomatoes
1 package (10 ounces) frozen
    peas
1 cup sliced fresh mushrooms
¾ cup dry red wine
¼ cup chopped fresh
    parsley
1 teaspoon sugar
1 teaspoon salt
⅛ teaspoon pepper
2 cups grated Parmesan
    cheese, divided

Cook macaroni according to chart on page 129. Drain and set aside. In 2-quart microproof casserole or bowl, combine meat and onions. Cook, covered, on HI (max. power) 3 minutes. Stir. Cook on HI (max. power) another 2 minutes, or until onion is transparent. Drain off fat. Add undrained tomatoes. With spoon, break up whole tomatoes into pieces. Add peas, mushrooms, wine, parsley, sugar, salt, and pepper. Cook, covered, on 50 (simmer) 30 minutes. In 13 × 9-inch microproof baking dish, layer half the sauce, half of the cooked macaroni, and 1 cup of cheese. Add remaining macaroni and sauce. Top with remaining cheese. Cover with waxed paper and cook on 60 (bake) 10 to 12 minutes, or until cheese is melted and casserole is bubbling. Let stand 5 minutes before serving.

6 to 8 servings

Vegetarian Macaroni

Total Cooking Time: 56 to 65 minutes

3 cups hot water
1 package (7 ounces) shell
    macaroni
3 tablespoons olive oil
1 large onion, sliced
2 cups sliced carrots
1 cup chopped celery
1 clove garlic, crushed
2 cups peeled, cubed
    tomatoes
½ teaspoon sage
½ teaspoon oregano
¼ teaspoon pepper
¼ teaspoon basil
⅛ teaspoon thyme
⅛ teaspoon rosemary
2 cans (16 ounces each)
    kidney beans, drained
    Salt and pepper
    Grated Parmesan cheese

In large microproof bowl, cook 3 cups hot water on HI (max. power) 6 to 8 minutes, or until boiling. Add macaroni, cover with waxed paper. Cook on HI (max. power) 1 minute. Let stand 5 minutes. Drain and set aside. In 4-quart microproof casserole, cook oil on HI (max. power) 2 minutes. Stir in onion, carrots, celery, and garlic. Continue cooking on HI (max. power) 10 to 12 minutes, or until vegetables are tender. Stir in tomatoes and seasonings. Cook, covered on 70 (roast) 7 minutes. Blend in macaroni and beans. Cook, covered, on HI (max. power) 12 to 15 minutes. Stir. Cook on 70 (roast) 18 to 20 minutes, stirring occasionally. Season with salt and pepper. Sprinkle with Parmesan cheese.

8 servings

Here is a spicy variation: Substitute ½ teaspoon cumin and ½ teaspoon chili powder for sage and oregano. Also substitute cayenne pepper for black pepper and use chili (pinto) beans for kidney beans. Olé — Mexican Macaroni!

Garlic Parmesan Bread (page 163), Macaroni Supreme →

Chinese Fried Rice

Total Cooking Time: 13 to 14 minutes

2 tablespoons butter or
  margarine
¼ cup thinly sliced green
  onion
3 cups cooked rice
½ teaspoon salt
1 tablespoon soy sauce
3 eggs
1 tablespoon water
¼ teaspoon sugar

Place butter and onion in 3-quart microproof casserole. Cook on HI (max. power) 4 minutes, or until onion is limp. Stir in rice, salt, and soy sauce. In small bowl beat eggs, water, and sugar just until mixed. Pour into center of rice. Cook, covered, on 70 (roast) 9 to 10 minutes, or until eggs are set and rice is dry in appearance. Stir eggs into rice after 3 minutes, then stir every 3 minutes until done.

4 to 6 servings

All Seasons Rice

Total Cooking Time: 12 to 14 minutes

2 cups chicken or beef
  broth
1 cup long-grained converted
  rice
¼ cup minced onion
2 tablespoons minced fresh
  parsley

Combine all ingredients in 2-quart glass casserole. Cover and cook on HI (max. power) 12 to 14 minutes. Let stand, covered, 10 minutes, or until all broth is absorbed.

4 servings

Low Calorie Rice Crust

Total Cooking Time: 1 minute

1½ cups cooked rice
1 egg
⅓ cup shredded Cheddar
  cheese

Combine ingredients and press evenly over bottom and sides of 9-inch glass pie plate or quiche dish. It is not necessary to cook before adding filling. However, if you prefer, cook on 70 (roast) 1 minute, or until cheese is melted.

Artichoke Pilaf

Total Cooking Time: 5½ minutes

2 jars (6 ounces each)
  marinated artichoke
  hearts
1 cup chopped onion
1 clove garlic, minced
½ cup thinly sliced celery
1 cup chicken broth
1 cup cooked rice
⅓ cup minced fresh
  parsley
½ teaspoon salt
⅛ teaspoon pepper

Drain artichokes, reserving 3 tablespoons marinade. In 2-quart microproof dish, place the reserved marinade, onion, garlic, and celery. Cook on HI (max. power) 2½ minutes, or until onion is transparent. Stir in remaining ingredients, including artichokes. Cook, covered, on HI (max. power) 3 minutes, stirring once during cooking. Let stand, uncovered, 5 minutes before serving.

4 to 6 servings.

Your microwave oven enables you to enter one of the most exciting areas of the culinary arts: the world of succulent crisp-cooked vegetables. Because very little water is used, sometimes none at all, vegetables emerge from the microwave oven with bright, fresh color, full of flavor, tender and nutritious. Even reheated, fresh vegetables retain their original flavor and color. They do not dry out, because the steam that heats them is primarily generated within the vegetables themselves. Canned vegetables heat well too, because they can be drained before cooking so that they retain their full fresh taste after cooking.

Arrange asparagus with the tender tips over-lapped in the center of the dish. Carrots cook a bit more quickly and are more interesting when cut diagonally (above). The husk on corn makes a natural wrapper. Just soak the corn in water for 5 minutes and then cook as directed on page 139 (above right). For best results, when cutting vegetables for cooking make sizes as uniform as possible (right).

Converting Your Recipes

Vegetables are best when eaten at the crisp stage, tender but resilient to the bite. However, if you prefer a softer texture, increase water and cooking time. To adapt a conventional recipe to the microwave oven, find a similar recipe in the chapter and check the vegetable cooking guides. The following tips will give you additional help in adapting or creating your own recipes:

- ☐ Check doneness after the shortest recommended cooking times. Add more cooking time to suit individual preferences.
- ☐ When using the temperature probe, a small amount of liquid should be added. Insert probe into the center of the vegetable dish and set at 150°F.
- ☐ If necessary, frozen vegetables may be used in recipes calling for fresh vegetables. It is not necessary to thaw frozen vegetables before cooking.
- ☐ Freeze small portions of your favorite vegetable dishes in boilable plastic pouches. If you use metal twist ties, be sure to replace with string or rubber band before cooking. Cut a steam vent in pouch and reheat on microproof plate.
- ☐ To prevent boiling over when preparing vegetable dishes with cream sauces, use a baking dish large enough to allow for bubbling. Use a lower power setting such as 60 or 70.
- ☐ Celery, onions, green peppers, and carrots need to be partially cooked before adding to a casserole. In general, you should partially cook all vegetables before combining with already cooked meats, fish, or poultry.
- ☐ To cook mashed potatoes, cube potatoes. Add a small amount of water. Cook, tightly covered, until soft. Season and mash.
- ☐ To reheat mashed potatoes, set at 80, stirring once during cooking time.
- ☐ Because carrots and beets are dense, they require more water and a longer cooking period to prevent dehydration and toughening during cooking.

Using the Cooking Guide

1. All fresh or frozen vegetables are cooked and reheated on HI (max. power).
2. Choose a wide, shallow dish so vegetables can be spread out.
3. Add ¼ cup water for each ½ to 1 pound fresh vegetables. Do not add water for washed spinach, corn on the cob, squash, baking potatoes, or eggplant.
4. Do not salt vegetables until after cooking.
5. Cover all vegetables tightly.
6. Stir vegetables once during cooking time.
7. Pouches of frozen vegetables require steam vents. Slit pouch and cook on microproof dish.
8. Frozen vegetables without sauces can be cooked in their cartons without water. Remove waxed paper wrapping before placing carton in oven. (Remove frozen-in-sauce vegetables if packaged in cartons rather than pouches. Place in 1½-quart microproof casserole. Add liquid before cooking as package directs.)
9. After cooking, allow all vegetables to stand, covered, for 2 to 3 minutes.

COOKING GUIDE — VEGETABLES

Food	Amount	Fresh Vegetable Preparation	Time (in minutes)	Water	Standing Time (in minutes)	Special Notes
Artichokes 3½" in diameter	Fresh: 1 2 4	Wash thoroughly. Cut tops off each leaf.	7-8 11-12	¼ cup ½ cup	2-3 2-3	When done, a leaf peeled from whole comes off easily.
	Frozen: 10 oz.	Slit pouch	5-6			
Asparagus: spears and cut pieces	Fresh: 1 lb.	Wash thoroughly. Snap off tough base and discard.	2-3	¼ cup	None	Stir or rearrange once during cooking time.
	Frozen: 10 oz.		7-8	None	2-3	
Beans: green, wax, French-cut	Fresh: 1 lb.	Remove ends. Wash well. Leave whole or break in pieces.	12-14	¼ cup	2-3	Stir once or rearrange as necessary.
	Frozen: 10 oz.		7-8	None	None	
Beets	4 medium	Scrub beets. Leave 1" of top on beet.	16-18	¼ cup	None	After cooking, peel. Cut or leave whole.
Broccoli	Fresh, whole 1-1½ lbs.	Remove outer leaves. Slit stalks.	9-10	¼ cup	3	Stir or rearrange during cooking time.
	Frozen, whole		8-10	¼ cup	3	
	Fresh, chopped, 1-1½ lbs.		12-14	¼ cup	2	
	Frozen, chopped 10 oz.		8-9	None	2	
Brussels sprouts	Fresh: 1 lb.	Remove outside leaves if wilted. Cut off stems. Wash	8-9	¼ cup	2-3	Stir or rearrange once during cooking time.
	Frozen: 10 oz.		6-7	None	None	
Cabbage	½ medium head, shredded	Remove outside wilted leaves.	5-6	¼ cup	2-3	
	1 medium head, wedges		13-15	¼ cup	2-3	Rearrange wedges after 7 minutes.
Carrots	4: sliced or diced	Peel and cut off tops.	7-9	1 Tb.	2-3	Stir once during cooking time.
	6: sliced or diced	Fresh young carrots cook best.	9-10	2 Tbs.	2-3	
	8: tiny, whole		8-10	2 Tbs.	2-3	
	Frozen: 10 oz.		8-9	None	None	
Cauliflower	1 medium, in flowerets	Cut tough stem. Wash, remove outside leaves. Remove core.	7-8	¼ cup	2-3	Stir after 5 minutes.
	1 medium, whole		8-9	½ cup	3	Turn over once.
	Frozen: 10 oz.		8-9	¼ cup	3	Stir after 5 minutes.
Celery	2½ cups, 1" slices	Clean stalks thoroughly.	8-9	¼ cup	2	
Corn: kernel	Frozen: 10 oz.		5-6	¼ cup	2	Stir halfway through cooking time.
On the cob	1 ear 2 ears 3 ears 4 ears	Husk, wrap each in waxed paper. Place on glass tray in oven. Cook no more than 4 at a time.	3-4 6-7 9-10 11-12	None None None None	2 2 2 2	Rearrange halfway through cooking time unless cooked on microproof rack.
	Frozen, 2 ears 4 ears	Flat dish, covered.	5½-6 10-11	None None	2	Rearrange halfway through cooking time.
Eggplant	1 medium, sliced	Wash and peel. Cut into slices or cubes.	5-6	2 Tb.	3	
	1 medium, whole	Pierce skin.	6-7			Place on micro-proof rack.
Greens: collard, kale, etc.	Fresh: 1 lb.	Wash. Remove wilted leaves or tough stem.	6-7	None	2	
	Frozen: 10 oz.		7-8	None	2	

COOKING GUIDE — VEGETABLES

Food	Amount	Fresh Vegetable Preparation	Time (in minutes)	Water	Standing Time (in minutes)	Special Notes
Mushrooms	Fresh: ½ lb., sliced	Add butter or water.	2 - 4	2 Tbs.		Stir halfway through cooking time.
Okra	Fresh: ½ lb.	Wash thoroughly. Leave whole or cut in thick slices.	3 - 5	¼ cup	2	
	Frozen: 10 oz.		7 - 8	None	2	
Onions	1 lb., tiny whole	Peel. Add 1 Tb. butter.	6 - 7	¼ cup	3	Stir once during cooking time.
	1 lb., medium to large	Peel and quarter. Add 1 Tb. butter.	7 - 9	¼ cup	3	
Parsnips	4 medium, quartered	Peel and cut.	8 - 9	¼ cup	2	Stir once during cooking time.
Peas: green	Fresh: 1 lb.	Shell peas. Rinse well.	7 - 8	¼ cup	2	Stir once during cooking time.
	Fresh: 2 lbs.		8 - 9	½ cup	2 - 3	
	Frozen: 10 oz.		5 - 6	None	None	
Peas and onions	Frozen: 10 oz.		6 - 8	2 Tbs.	2	
Pea pods	Frozen: 6 oz.		3 - 4	2 Tbs.	3	
Potatoes, sweet 5 - 6 oz. ea.	1	Scrub well. Pierce with fork. Place on rack or paper towel in circle, 1" apart.	4 - 4½	None	3	
	2		6 - 7	None	3	
	4		8 - 10	None	3	
	6		10 - 11	None	3	
Potatoes, white baking 6 - 8 oz. ea.	1	Wash and scrub well. Pierce with fork. Place on rack or paper towel in circle, 1" apart.	4 - 6	None	3	
	2		6 - 8	None	3	
	3		8 - 12	None	3	
	4		12 - 16	None	3	
	5		16 - 20	None	3	
russet, boiling	3	Peel potatoes, cut in quarters.	12 - 16	½ cup	None	Stir once during cooking time.
Rutabaga	Fresh: 1 lb.	Wash well. Remove tough stems or any wilted leaves.	6 - 7	None	2	Stir once during cooking time.
	Frozen: 10 oz.		7 - 8	None	2	
Spinach	Fresh: 1 lb.	Wash well. Remove tough stems. Drain.	6 - 7	None	2	Stir once during cooking time.
	Frozen: 10 oz.		7 - 8	None	2	
Squash, acorn or butternut	1 - 1½ lbs. whole	Scrub. Pierce with fork.	10 - 12	None		Cut and remove seeds to serve.
Spaghetti squash	2 - 3 lbs.	Scrub, pierce. Place on rack.	6 per lb.	None	5	Serve with butter, Parmesan cheese, or spaghetti sauce.
Turnips	4 cups cubed	Peel, wash.	9 - 11	¼ cup	3	Stir after 5 minutes.
Zucchini	3 cups sliced	Wash; do not peel.	7 - 8	¼ cup	2	Stir after 4 minutes.

COOKING GUIDE — CANNED VEGETABLES

Size	Cook Control Setting	Minutes Drained	Minutes Undrained	Special Notes
8 ounces	80 (reheat)	1½ - 2	2 - 2½	Regardless of quantity: use a 4-cup microproof casserole, covered. Stir once. Let stand, covered, 2 - 3 minutes before serving.
15 ounces	80 (reheat)	2½ - 3	3 - 4	
17 ounces	80 (reheat)	3½ - 4	4 - 5	

Note: Temperature probe may be used. Set Cook Control on 80 (reheat). Temperature control at 150°. Place probe in center of dish. Stir halfway through cooking time.

COOKING GUIDE — CONVENIENCE VEGETABLES

Food	Amount	Cook Control Setting	Time (in minutes)	or	Temperature Probe Setting	Special Notes
Au gratin vegetables, frozen	11½ oz.	70 (roast)	10-12		150°	Use glass loaf dish, covered.
Baked beans, frozen	6 oz.	70 (roast)	8-10		150°	Use 1½-quart casserole, covered. Stir once.
Corn, scalloped frozen	12 oz.	70 (roast)	7-8		150°	Use 1-quart casserole, covered.
Potatoes stuffed, frozen	2	70 (roast)	10-12			Use shallow dish. Cover with waxed paper.
Tots, frozen	16 oz. 32 oz.	80 (reheat) 80 (reheat)	9-10 12-14			Use 2-quart round or oval baking dish. Rearrange once.
Creamed potato mix	4-5 oz.	70 (roast)	20-24		150°	
Au gratin, frozen	11½ oz.	70 (roast)	12			Use 1½-quart casserole, covered with waxed paper.
Instant mashed	3½ oz. packet	HI (max. power)	5-6			Use covered casserole. Follow package directions. Reduce liquid by 1 tablespoon.
Peas, pea pods, chestnuts, frozen	10 oz.	HI (max. power)	6-7			Place pouch on plate. Slit pouch. Flex once during cooking time to mix.
Stuffing mix	6 oz.	HI (max. power)	8			Use 1½-quart casserole, covered. Follow package directions.

Note: When cooking vegetables, use temperature probe only after vegetables are thawed. For frozen soufflés, see chart on page 119.

Using the Blanching Guide

The microwave oven can be a valuable and appreciated aid in preparing fresh vegetables for the freezer. (The oven is *not* recommended for canning.) Some vegetables don't require any water at all and, of course, the less water used the better. You'll have that "fresh picked" color and flavor for your produce. Here are some tips in preparing vegetables for blanching:

☐ Choose young, tender vegetables.
☐ Clean and prepare for cooking according to Cooking Guide.
☐ Measure amounts to be blanched; place by batches, in microproof casserole.
☐ Add water according to chart.
☐ Cover and cook on HI (max. power) for time indicated on chart.
☐ Stir vegetables halfway through cooking.
☐ Let vegetables stand, covered, 1 minute after cooking.
☐ Place vegetables in ice water at once to stop cooking. When vegetables feel cool, spread on towel to absorb excess moisture.
☐ Package in freezer containers or pouches. Seal, label, date, and freeze quickly.

BLANCHING GUIDE — VEGETABLES

Food	Amount	Water	Approximate Time (in minutes)	Casserole Size
Asparagus (cut in 1-inch pieces)	4 cups	¼ cup	4½	1½ quart
Beans, green or wax (cut in 1-inch pieces)	1 pound	½ cup	5	1½ quart
Broccoli (cut in 1-inch pieces)	1 pound	⅓ cup	6	1½ quart
Carrots (sliced)	1 pound	⅓ cup	6	1½ quart
Cauliflower (cut in flowerets)	1 head	⅓ cup	6	2 quart
Corn (cut from cob)	4 cups	none	4	1½ quart
Corn-on-the-cob (husked)	6 ears	none	5½	1½ quart
Onion (quartered)	4 medium	½ cup	3 - 4½	1 quart
Parsnips (cubed)	1 pound	¼ cup	2½ - 4	1½ quart
Peas (shelled)	4 cups	¼ cup	4½	1½ quart
Snow peas	4 cups	¼ cup	3½	1½ quart
Spinach (washed)	1 pound	none	4	2 quart
Turnips (cubed)	1 pound	¼ cup	3 - 4½	1½ quart
Zucchini (sliced or cubed)	1 pound	¼ cup	4	1½ quart

Spinach Oriental
Total Cooking Time: 4 to 5 minutes

10 ounces spinach, washed, torn into bite-size pieces
1 can (8 ounces) sliced water chestnuts, drained
4 green onions, sliced
2 tablespoons vegetable oil
2 tablespoons wine vinegar
2 tablespoons soy sauce
1 teaspoon sugar

In 2-quart microproof casserole place spinach, water chestnuts, and onions. Cook, covered, on HI (max. power) 3 to 4 minutes, or until spinach is limp. Stir, set aside covered. In 1-cup glass measure place oil, vinegar, soy sauce, and sugar. Cook on HI (max. power) 1 minute. Pour over spinach, toss, and serve hot.

4 servings

Sweet-Sour Red Cabbage
Total Cooking Time: 23 to 27 minutes

1½ pounds red cabbage
1 tart apple, peeled, cored, and diced
1 tablespoon butter or margarine
5 tablespoons red wine vinegar
1 teaspoon salt
3 tablespoons sugar

Shred cabbage into 3-quart microproof casserole. Add apple, butter, and vinegar. Stir. Cook, covered, on HI (max. power) 18 to 22 minutes, or until apples and cabbage are tender. Stir twice during cooking time. Stir in salt and sugar. Cook, covered, on HI (max. power) 5 minutes, or until liquid comes to a boil.

6 servings

Peas Francine

Total Cooking Time: 9 to 10 minutes

In 1½-quart glass casserole place peas, water, and sugar. Stir. Cook, covered, on HI (max. power) 4 minutes. Stir and cover surface with lettuce, overlapping as necessary. Cook, covered, on HI (max. power) 5 to 6 minutes, or until tender. Remove lettuce leaves and discard; drain peas. Stir in salt and pepper. Cover and let stand 2 to 3 minutes before serving.

4 servings

2 cups fresh shelled peas
¼ cup water
1 teaspoon sugar
3 or 4 large lettuce leaves
Dash salt and pepper

Sautéed Mushrooms

Total Cooking Time: 4 to 5 minutes

Clean and slice mushrooms. Place in 8-inch microproof dish. Add garlic and butter. Cover with waxed paper and cook on 90 (sauté) 4 to 5 minutes, stirring once after 2 minutes.

2 to 4 servings

½ pound mushrooms
1 clove garlic, minced
¼ cup butter or margarine

Serve with roast beef or steak, or as a "surprise" side dish with any meal. Sautéed mushrooms also make a fine main dish, served on toast, and sprinkled with Parmesan cheese.

Ratatouille

Total Cooking Time: 22 to 24 minutes

Place eggplant on microproof rack, pierce well with fork. Cook on HI (max. power) 7 minutes. Set aside to cool. In 2½-quart glass casserole, combine olive oil, garlic, and onion. Cook, covered, on HI (max. power) 4 minutes, or until onion is limp. Stir in zucchini and green pepper. Peel eggplant and cut into 1½-inch cubes (about 2 cups). Add to zucchini mixture, stir well. Cook, covered, on HI (max. power) 5 minutes. Stir in tomatoes, basil, salt, thyme, and pepper. Cook, uncovered, on HI (max. power) 6 to 8 minutes, or until vegetables are tender. Sprinkle with Parmesan cheese.

6 to 8 servings

1 eggplant (1½ pounds)
¼ cup olive oil
2 cloves garlic, minced
1 medium onion, sliced
3 medium (1 pound) zucchini, sliced (about 3 cups)
1 green pepper, cut into strips
4 firm tomatoes, chopped
1 teaspoon basil
1 teaspoon salt
Pinch thyme, crumbled
¼ teaspoon pepper
¼ cup minced fresh parsley
2 tablespoons grated Parmesan cheese

Harvard Beets

Total Cooking Time: 7½ to 8 minutes

Drain beets, reserving liquid. In 1-cup glass measure, pour beet liquid and add enough water to make 1 cup of liquid. In 1-quart microproof casserole or bowl, combine sugar, cornstarch, salt, pepper, and vinegar. Stir in beet liquid. Cook, uncovered, on HI (max. power) 2½ to 3 minutes, stirring occasionally, until mixture thickens and is clear. Add beets and stir lightly. Cook, covered, on HI (max. power) about 5 minutes, or until beets are hot.

4 servings

1 can (16 ounces) diced or sliced beets
¼ cup sugar
1 tablespoon cornstarch
½ teaspoon salt
⅛ teaspoon pepper
¼ cup wine vinegar

Crumb Topped Tomatoes

Total Cooking Time: 3½ to 4½ minutes

Cut slice off stem end of each tomato and discard. Place tomatoes, cut side up, in circle on microproof plate. Combine onion soup mix, melted butter, crumbs, parsley, and basil. Divide among 4 tomatoes, spreading mixture on cut surface. Cook, uncovered, on HI (max. power) 3½ to 4½ minutes, or until tomatoes are hot.

4 servings

4 medium tomatoes
1 tablespoon dry onion soup mix
1½ tablespoons butter or margarine, melted
1½ tablespoons dry bread crumbs
1 tablespoon chopped fresh parsley
1 tablespoon chopped fresh basil, or 1 teaspoon dried basil

Country Style Potatoes

Total Cooking Time: 18 to 21 minutes

Place potatoes in 2-quart microproof casserole with water. Cook, covered, on HI (max. power) 10 to 12 minutes, or until steaming hot. Drain. Add milk, salt, chives, and butter. Stir carefully, then stir in Parmesan cheese and sprinkle with paprika. Cook, uncovered, on 50 (simmer) 8 to 9 minutes, or until tender.

6 servings

5 medium potatoes, peeled and shredded (about 6 cups)
¼ cup water
1½ cups whole milk
1 teaspoon salt
¼ cup chopped chives
¼ cup butter or margarine, cut up
¼ cup grated Parmesan cheese
  Paprika

1 package (24 ounces) frozen shredded hash browns may be substituted for raw potatoes. Heat in package on HI (max. power) 10 to 12 minutes, turning once during cooking time. Empty potatoes into 2-quart casserole and continue as directed.

← *Harvard Beets*

Baked Acorn Squash

Total Cooking Time: 15 to 17 minutes

⅓ cup butter or margarine
2 acorn squash (1 pound each)
½ cup fine bread crumbs
⅓ cup chopped walnuts
3 tablespoons brown sugar, packed
½ teaspoon salt
¼ teaspoon nutmeg

In 2-cup glass measure melt butter on HI (max. power) 1 minute. Wash squash, pierce, and place on microproof plate. Cook on HI (max. power) 2 minutes. Cut in half lengthwise. Remove seeds and fibers. Place cut side down on 12×7×2-inch microproof baking dish. Cook on HI (max. power) 6 minutes. While squash is cooking, add remaining ingredients to melted butter, and mix well. Turn squash cut side up, divide crumb mixture among 4 halves. Cook, covered, on HI (max. power) 6 to 8 minutes, or until squash is tender. Remove cover and let stand 5 minutes before serving.

4 servings

Creamy Cabbage

Total Cooking Time: 8 to 10 minutes

1 medium head cabbage
¼ cup water
1 package (3 ounces) cream cheese, cubed
2 tablespoons milk
½ teaspoon salt
½ teaspoon celery seed
   Dash pepper
   Paprika

Shred cabbage into 2-quart microproof casserole. Add water. Cook, covered, on HI (max. power) 7 to 9 minutes, or until done. Stir once during cooking time. Add all remaining ingredients except paprika. Cook, covered, on HI (max. power) 1 minute. Stir carefully to mix cheese with cabbage. Garnish with paprika.

5 to 6 servings

Corn and Pepper Pudding

Total Cooking Time: 18 to 19 minutes

2 tablespoons butter or margarine
2 tablespoons chopped green pepper
2 tablespoons chopped pimiento
1 tablespoon minced instant onion
3 tablespoons all-purpose flour
1 teaspoon salt
¼ teaspoon pepper
2 eggs, slightly beaten
¼ cup milk
2 cans (16½ ounces each) cream-style corn

Place butter, green pepper, and pimiento in shallow 1½-quart round or oval microproof dish. Cook on 90 (sauté) 2 minutes. Stir in remaining ingredients, mixing well. Cook, covered, on 70 (roast) 9 minutes. Stir and cook, uncovered, on 70 (roast) 7 to 8 minutes, or until pudding is set. The center will be slightly soft. Let stand 5 minutes before serving.

6 servings

Corn-Mushroom Scallop
Total Cooking Time: 8 to 9 minutes

In 1-quart glass casserole, mix well corn, mushrooms, and egg. Stir in ½ cup of cracker crumbs, chives, and pepper. Spread evenly in casserole and sprinkle with remaining ¼ cup of crumbs. Dot crumbs with butter. Cook on HI (max. power) 8 to 9 minutes, or until set in center. Allow to stand 5 minutes before serving.

4 servings

1 can (16½ ounces) cream-style corn
¼ pound mushrooms, sliced
1 egg, slightly beaten
¾ cup soda cracker crumbs, divided
1 tablespoon chopped chives
¼ teaspoon white pepper
2 tablespoons butter or margarine

Candied Sweet Potatoes
Total Cooking Time: 19 to 22 minutes

Cook sweet potatoes according to chart on page 140. Peel and slice. Arrange in 2-quart microproof casserole. Set aside. In 2-cup glass measure combine sugar, butter, water, and salt. Cook, uncovered, on 70 (roast) 3 to 4 minutes, stirring once. Pour over potato slices. Cook, covered, on HI (max. power) 7 to 8 minutes, or until heated through. Spoon glaze over potatoes at least once during cooking.

6 servings

To prepare two servings, cook 2 potatoes, slice into small casserole. Combine in 1-cup glass measure ⅓ cup brown sugar, 2 teaspoons butter, 2 tablespoons water, and dash of salt. Cook on 70 (roast) 1 to 1½ minutes. Pour over sliced potatoes. Cook, covered, on 70 (roast) 2½ to 3 minutes.

5 sweet potatoes (5 to 6 ounces each)
1 cup brown sugar, firmly packed
2 tablespoons butter or margarine
⅓ cup water
½ teaspoon salt

Savory Cauliflower
Total Cooking Time: 10 minutes

Cut cone-shaped wedge out of cauliflower core. Place cauliflower and water in 1½-quart microproof casserole. Cook, covered, on HI (max. power) 9 minutes. Turn over halfway. Drain. Mix mayonnaise, onion, mustard, and salt. Spoon sauce over top of cauliflower. Lay cheese slices on top. Cook, uncovered, on 70 (roast) 1 minute, or until cheese is melted. Sprinkle with paprika. Let stand 2 minutes before serving.

6 servings

1 medium head cauliflower
¼ cup water
½ cup mayonnaise or salad dressing
1 tablespoon instant minced onion
½ teaspoon dry mustard
¼ teaspoon salt
4 slices Colby cheese
Paprika

Twice-Baked Potatoes
Total Cooking Time: 16 to 20 minutes

4 baking potatoes (4 to 5
   ounces each)
½ cup butter or margarine,
   cut up
½ cup dairy sour cream
½ teaspoon salt
   Dash pepper
   Paprika

Pierce potatoes and place on a paper towel, in oven, in a circle about 1 inch apart. Cook on HI (max. power) 12 to 16 minutes. Potatoes may feel firm when done; let stand to soften. Do not overcook, as potatoes will dehydrate. Remove ¼-inch horizontal slice from top of each potato. Using teaspoon, remove centers to a mixing bowl. (Leave shells intact.) Add sour cream, salt, and pepper to potato pulp and beat vigorously until smooth. Divide mixture evenly in shells, mounding if necessary. Place potatoes in circle on microproof plate. Cook on HI (max. power) 4 minutes. Sprinkle with paprika.

4 servings

Green Beans Italian
Total Cooking Time: 15 to 17 minutes

3 slices bacon
2 packages (10 ounces each)
   frozen green beans
¼ cup water
1 small onion, thickly
   sliced
¾ cup bottled Italian
   dressing

Cook bacon according to directions on page 71. Place green beans with water in 1½-quart microproof casserole. Cook, covered, on HI (max. power) 9 to 10 minutes, or until almost tender, stirring once during cooking time. Add onion and Italian dressing. Cook, covered, on HI (max. power) 3 to 4 minutes, or until beans are tender and onion is transparent. Sprinkle with crumbled cooked bacon.

6 servings

Cranberry Carrots
Total Cooking Time: 13 to 14 minutes

6 carrots, sliced, or 1
   package (10 ounces)
   frozen sliced carrots
¼ cup butter or margarine
¼ cup jellied cranberry sauce
   Salt

Cook carrots according to chart on page 139. Set aside. Place butter in 1½ to 2-quart microproof casserole. Cook, covered, on HI (max. power) 1 minute, or until butter is melted. Add cranberry sauce. Cook, covered, on HI (max. power) 1 minute, or until cranberry sauce is melted. Stir and mix in cooked carrots. Cook on HI (max. power) 2 minutes. Season to taste.

4 servings

Twice-Baked Potatoes, Green Beans Italian, →
Cranberry Carrots

Pan Baked Potato Halves

Total Cooking Time: 10¾ to 12¾ minutes

2 tablespoons butter or
 margarine
¼ cup grated Parmesan cheese
½ teaspoon salt
¼ teaspoon white pepper
4 medium potatoes (4 to 5
 ounces each)
 Paprika

In small glass bowl melt butter on HI (max. power) 45 seconds. In separate bowl mix cheese and seasonings. Cut washed potatoes in half lengthwise. Dip cut side in butter, then in cheese mixture. Place potato halves cut side up in 2-quart baking dish. Cook on HI (max. power) 10 to 12 minutes, or until tender. Let stand 5 minutes. Sprinkle cut side with paprika and serve hot.

8 servings

Italian bread crumbs or corn flake crumbs may be substituted for Parmesan cheese.

Parsley New Potatoes

Total Cooking Time: 10 to 12 minutes

12 (1 pound) small
 new potatoes
¼ cup water
2 tablespoons butter,
 melted
1 tablespoon minced fresh
 parsley
 Dash salt and pepper

Wash potatoes. Cut a ½-inch strip from middle of each. Place in 2-quart microproof casserole, add water, cover. Cook on HI (max. power) 10 to 12 minutes. Stir once during cooking. Drain and stir in butter, parsley, salt and pepper. Serve hot.

4 servings

Broccoli-Carrot Casserole

Total Cooking Time: 9¾ to 10¾ minutes

1 package (10 ounces) frozen
 broccoli spears
1 can (10¾ ounces) cream
 of chicken soup
½ cup dairy sour cream
1 cup finely shredded carrots
1 tablespoon all-purpose
 flour
1 tablespoon minced onion
¼ teaspoon salt
⅛ teaspoon pepper
2 tablespoons butter or
 margarine
¾ cup herb-seasoned stuffing
 cubes

Defrost broccoli in package on paper towel at HI (max. power) 2 minutes, or until you can separate spears. Set aside. In 1½-quart microproof casserole, mix soup, sour cream, carrots, flour, onion, salt, and pepper. Cut broccoli in one-inch pieces and stir into soup mixture. Cook, covered, on HI (max. power) 3 minutes. Stir carefully. Place butter in 2-cup glass measure and cook on HI (max. power) 45 seconds, or until melted. Stir in stuffing and spoon over broccoli. Cook, uncovered, on HI (max. power) 4 to 5 minutes, or until hot.

5 to 6 servings

Sauces are a cinch in your microwave oven. No scorching, less stirring, and quick results. Sauces don't stick or burn as they do on the conventional range. They heat evenly and require less time and attention. You don't have to stir constantly or use a double boiler. Just an occasional stir is all that is required to prevent lumping, and, if you like, a little beating after cooking will make a sauce velvet smooth. You can measure, mix, and cook all in the same cup, or in the serving pitcher itself. Try making a sauce the microwave way, and turn an ordinary food into an elegant treat.

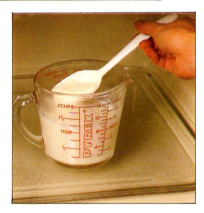

Sauces are so easy! Steps in making Basic White Sauce (below) are illustrated.

Basic White Sauce

Total Cooking Time: 6¾ to 7¾ minutes

In 2-cup glass measure, heat milk on 70 (roast) 2 minutes. Set aside. In 2-cup glass measure, melt butter on HI (max. power) 45 seconds. Stir in flour, cook on HI (max. power) 1 minute. Briskly stir in warm milk, pepper, and nutmeg. Cook on HI (max. power) 3 to 4 minutes, or until boiling, stirring once during cooking. Let stand 5 minutes before serving. Serve with cooked broccoli and cauliflower, or use as base for other sauces.

1 cup milk
2 tablespoons butter or
    margarine
2 tablespoons all-purpose
    flour
    Dash white pepper
    Dash grated or ground
    nutmeg

1 cup

Converting Your Recipes

All those sauces generally considered too difficult for the average cook are easy in the microwave oven. When looking for a sauce recipe similar to the conventional one you want to convert, find a recipe with a similar quantity of liquid and similar main thickening ingredient such as cornstarch, flour, egg, cheese, or jelly. Read the directions carefully to determine procedure, timing, and cook control setting. Then, when you stir, notice the progress of the sauce, and remove when the right consistency or doneness is reached. Keep notes to help you the next time. The following tips will help:

☐ Use a microproof container about twice the volume of ingredients to safeguard against the sauce boiling over — so easy with milk- and cream-based sauces.

☐ Sauces and salad dressings with ingredients not sensitive to high heat should be cooked on HI (max. power). Basic White Sauce and Lemon Butter Sauce are examples.

☐ Bring flour and other starch-thickened mixtures to a boil and remove as soon as thickened. Remember, overcooking will destroy thickening agent and sauce will thin.

☐ You will notice that more flour or cornstarch is required in microwave cooking than in conventional cooking to thicken sauces and gravies, since they will not be reduced by evaporation.

☐ Stirring quickly two or three times during cooking is sufficient to ensure even cooking. Too many stirrings may slow cooking.

☐ To reheat sauces: Dessert sauces to 125° with temperature probe. Main dish sauces, such as gravy or canned spaghetti sauce, to 150° with temperature probe.

☐ When sauces require time to develop flavor or if they contain eggs, which might curdle, they should be cooked slowly, on 50 (simmer) or even 30 (defrost). Don't allow delicate egg yolk sauces to boil.

☐ You can make your own special sauce by flavoring Basic White Sauce (page 151) as desired. For example, add cheese, cooked mushrooms, cooked onions, your favorite spices, tomato paste, horseradish, etc.

Hot Lemony Dill Sauce

Total Cooking Time: 3½ to 4½ minutes

½ cup butter or margarine
2 tablespoons all-purpose flour
1 teaspoon instant chicken bouillon
½ teaspoon dill weed
½ teaspoon salt
1 cup chicken broth
2 tablespoons lemon juice

In 2-cup glass measure, melt butter on HI (max. power) about 1½ minutes. Blend in flour, bouillon, dill weed, and salt. Briskly stir in broth and mix until blended. Cook on HI (max. power) 2 to 3 minutes, or until mixture boils and is thickened, stirring twice during cooking. Stir in lemon juice. Serve with broiled or poached salmon steaks.

1½ cups

Clarified Butter

Total Cooking Time: 1½ to 2½ minutes

In 2-cup glass measure, melt butter slowly on 20 (low) 1½ to 2½ minutes, or until completely melted and oil starts to separate but has not started to bubble. Let butter stand a few minutes, skim off foam. Slowly pour off yellow oil and reserve. This is the clarified butter. Discard the leftover impurities. Serve as dipping for steamed clams, crab legs, or shrimp.

⅓ cup

1 cup butter (½ pound)

Béarnaise Sauce

Total Cooking Time: 1 to 2 minutes

In blender container, place egg yolks, vinegar, onion, chervil, and pepper. In 1-cup glass measure, heat butter on HI (max. power) 1 to 2 minutes, or until bubbly. Turn blender to high speed and gradually add butter through cover opening. Blend until sauce is thick and creamy. Stir in parsley and serve warm. Serve on broiled steak, cooked green vegetables, poached eggs, or fish.

½ cup

4 egg yolks
2 teaspoons tarragon vinegar
1 teaspoon instant minced
   onion
½ teaspoon chervil
   Dash white pepper
½ cup butter
1 teaspoon minced fresh
   parsley

Lemon Butter Sauce

Total Cooking Time: 1½ to 2 minutes

Combine all ingredients in 2-cup glass measure. Cook, uncovered, on HI (max. power) 1½ to 2 minutes, or until hot and butter is melted. Stir. Serve immediately with seafood, hot green vegetables, Simple Salmon Loaf (page 115).

⅔ cup

2 tablespoons lemon juice
½ cup butter or margarine
⅛ teaspoon salt
⅛ teaspoon white pepper

Easy Gravy

Total Cooking Time: 3 to 4 minutes

Pour drippings into 4-cup glass measure. Stir in flour until smooth. Pour in liquid and stir briskly until well blended. Cook on HI (max. power) 3 to 4 minutes, or until boiling, stirring several times during cooking. Season with salt and pepper. Beat until smooth. Serve hot with meat, potatoes, or dressing.

2½ cups

¼ cup meat or poultry
   drippings (juice from
   meat with most of the
   fat removed)
¼ cup all-purpose flour
2 cups warm liquid (broth,
   water, or juice)
   Salt and pepper

Hollandaise Sauce

Total Cooking Time: 2 minutes

¼ cup butter or margarine
¼ cup light cream
2 egg yolks, well beaten
1 tablespoon lemon juice
½ teaspoon dry mustard
¼ teaspoon salt

In 4-cup glass measure, cook butter on HI (max. power) 1 minute, or until butter is melted. Add remaining ingredients. Beat with electric mixer or wire whisk until smooth. Cook on 70 (roast) 1 minute, beating well with whisk every 15 seconds until thickened. Remove from oven and beat with electric mixer or wire whisk until light and smooth. Serve immediately with cooked asparagus, broccoli, or Eggs Benedict (page 123).

¾ cup

If sauce curdles, beat in 1 teaspoon hot water and continue beating until mixture is smooth.

To reheat Hollandaise, heat on 20 (low) 15 to 30 seconds, stir, let stand 1 minute, and repeat until hot.

Raisin Brandy Sauce

Total Cooking Time: 4 to 6 minutes

½ cup raisins
¼ cup apple brandy
3 tablespoons brown sugar, firmly packed
1 tablespoon cornstarch
1 cup apple cider
2 tablespoons lemon juice
⅛ teaspoon ground cloves
⅛ teaspoon nutmeg

In small glass bowl, heat raisins and brandy on HI (max. power) 1 minute. Set aside. In 2-cup glass measure, mix sugar and cornstarch. Briskly stir in cider and lemon juice until blended. Cook on HI (max. power), 2 to 3 minutes, stirring every minute, or until thick and clear. Stir in cloves, nutmeg, and brandy-raisin mixture. Cook on HI (max. power) 1 to 2 minutes. Let stand 5 minutes. Serve warm with ham, beef tongue, baked squash, gingerbread, or baked apples.

1½ cups

Tarragon Sauce

Total Cooking Time: 4 minutes

½ cup unsalted butter
⅓ cup dry white wine
1 tablespoon tarragon vinegar
2 tablespoons minced fresh tarragon or 2 teaspoons dried tarragon
1 tablespoon chopped chives
½ teaspoon salt
¼ teaspoon pepper
Dash hot-pepper sauce
3 egg yolks

Place all ingredients except egg yolks in 2-cup glass measure; cook on HI (max. power) 2 minutes. Beat egg yolks in small bowl. Stir in small amount of butter mixture, then stir yolks into sauce. Cook on 50 (simmer) 2 minutes, stirring once. Beat until smooth. Serve immediately with poached eggs, broiled meats, hot cauliflower or carrots.

1 cup

Hollandaise Sauce on Asparagus, →
Raisin Brandy Sauce on Ham

Choco-Peanut Butter Sauce
Total Cooking Time: 2½ to 4 minutes

1 square (1 ounce) unsweetened baking chocolate
¼ cup milk
1 cup sugar
⅓ cup peanut butter
¼ teaspoon vanilla

In 4-cup glass measure, heat chocolate with milk on HI (max. power) 1½ to 2 minutes, or until chocolate is melted. Stir, then stir in sugar. Cook on HI (max. power) 1 to 2 minutes, or until mixture boils. Add peanut butter and vanilla. Stir until blended. Serve hot or cold over ice cream, cake, or sliced bananas.

1 cup

Rum Custard Sauce
Total Cooking Time: 9 to 11 minutes

1½ cups milk
½ cup light cream
⅓ cup sugar
⅛ teaspoon salt
3 eggs, lightly beaten
3 tablespoons rum

In 4-cup glass measure, heat milk, cream, sugar, and salt on 70 (roast) 3 to 4 minutes, or until the boiling point is reached. Mix ½ cup milk mixture and eggs. Stir into remaining milk mixture. Cook on 50 (simmer) 2 minutes; stir. Cook on 30 (defrost) 4 to 5 minutes, stirring every minute, until thickened. Cool to room temperature and stir in rum. Serve with bread pudding, banana pudding, poached peaches and pears.

2½ cups

Strawberry Sauce
Total Cooking Time: 3 to 4 minutes

1 pint fresh strawberries
½ cup sugar
2 tablespoons cornstarch
1 cup water
2 tablespoons butter or margarine
½ cup lemon juice

Clean and hull berries. Reserve a few of the best berries for garnish. Force the remainder through a food mill or blend in electric blender. Strain to remove seeds, set purée aside. In 4-cup glass measure, mix sugar and cornstarch, stir in water. Cook on HI (max. power) 3 to 4 minutes, or until mixture comes to a boil and is thick and clear. Stir twice during cooking. Add butter and stir until melted. Stir in lemon juice, butter, and strawberry purée. Chill. Serve on pound cake, over vanilla pudding, custard, or as a parfait sauce.

2½ cups

Choco-Peanut Butter Sauce on Ice Cream →
Rum Custard Sauce with Peaches,

Spicy Barbecue Sauce
Total Cooking Time: 5 minutes

1 can (8 ounces) tomato
   sauce
¼ cup wine vinegar
2 tablespoons brown sugar
2 tablespoons prepared mustard
1 tablespoon Worcestershire
   sauce
1 tablespoon instant minced
   onion
¼ teaspoon salt
1 teaspoon celery seed
1 clove garlic, minced
   (optional)
   Dash hot-pepper sauce

Combine all ingredients well in 4-cup glass measure. Cover with plastic wrap, cook on HI (max. power) 5 minutes, stirring once. Stir and let stand 5 minutes. Serve with Country Style Ribs (page 82), chicken, or pork chops.

1⅓ cups

This sauce can be used as a marinade before cooking to enhance the flavor of spareribs, pork, chicken, and lamb. Refrigerate marinated meats from 2 hours to 24 hours.

Best Ever French Dressing
Total Cooking Time: 8 to 10 minutes

½ cup lemon juice
¼ cup wine vinegar
1 small onion, sliced
1 clove garlic, split
¾ cup sugar
2 tablespoons corn syrup
½ cup water
½ cup catsup
1 cup vegetable oil
1 teaspoon salt
1 teaspoon paprika
1 teaspoon celery salt
1 teaspoon dry mustard

Mix lemon juice, vinegar, onion, and garlic in small bowl. Set aside while preparing other ingredients. In 4-cup glass measure boil sugar, syrup, and water on HI (max. power) 8 to 10 minutes, or until a soft ball forms when dropped in cold water. Cool syrup. Strain lemon-vinegar mixture and add to syrup. Discard garlic and onion. Add all other ingredients and beat with an egg beater or electric mixer until blended and thick. Refrigerate. Besides serving on green salad, use as a sauce for your favorite combination of raw or blanched vegetables.

2½ cups

Butterscotch Sauce
Total Cooking Time: 4½ to 5½ minutes

1½ tablespoons cornstarch
1¼ cups brown sugar, packed
½ cup light cream
2 tablespoons corn syrup
⅛ teaspoon salt
¼ cup butter or margarine
1 teaspoon vanilla

In 1½-quart casserole, stir together cornstarch and brown sugar. Stir in cream, corn syrup, salt; add butter. Cook, covered, on HI (max. power) 4½ to 5½ minutes, stirring after 2 minutes, until sugar is dissolved and sauce is thickened. Add vanilla and stir. Serve hot or cold, over ice cream or cake.

1½ cups

Treat your family and friends to the rich aromas of hot-from-the-oven bread, sweet rolls, muffins, and coffee cakes. For a quick and easy surprise breakfast or coffee break, count on the short cooking time of the microwave oven. Bread cooked in the microwave has an excellent texture and flavor, but does not brown or develop crust — there is no hot air to dry the surface as in conventional baking. For best results, if you like the browned look for your bread and muffins, use dark flours, molasses, and spices. Because a crust doesn't form, bread cooked in the microwave oven has the remarkable characteristic of rising higher than in conventional cooking. With tender, loving care you'll soon succeed in making homemade bread, muffins, and sweet rolls a constant addition to your menus.

Breads, such as Zucchini-Nut Bread (page 164), and cakes are tested for doneness just as in conventional cooking (above left). Custard cups arranged in a circle may be used to make muffins (above). Proofing bread is a snap. A cup of water helps provide a moist environment (left).

Converting Your Recipes

When adapting "quick bread" recipes you will find it necessary to reduce the amount of leavening (baking powder or soda) by about one-quarter the normal amount. A bitter aftertaste is apparent if too much leavening is used in biscuits or muffins. Since foods rise higher in the microwave oven, you will not see a loss in volume from the reduction of soda or baking powder. If a recipe contains buttermilk or sour cream, do not change the amount of soda, since it serves to counteract the sour taste and does not act only as a leavening agent. When using a mix where leavening cannot be reduced, if you allow the batter or dough to stand about 10 minutes before cooking, some of the gas will be lost. Yeast doughs need not be changed but may cook more evenly if cooked in a bundt or ring mold shape rather than the conventional loaf pan. And observe the following tips:

- ☐ Because breads rise higher than in a conventional oven, use a larger loaf pan to accommodate the volume.
- ☐ Fill paper-lined muffin cups only half full to allow for muffins rising more.
- ☐ You can prepare your own "brown 'n serve" breads and rolls by baking them ahead in the microwave oven. Then place them in the conventional oven to brown just before serving.
- ☐ Breads and rolls should be reheated to the point where they are warm to the touch. Overheating or overcooking makes bread tough and rubbery.
- ☐ Heat bread slices on paper napkins or paper towels to absorb excess moisture. You can heat bread and rolls on a microproof roasting rack as well. Or you can heat them on a paper napkin-lined basket and serve them right from the oven.
- ☐ When making yeast bread in a microwave oven, choose a recipe with cornmeal, whole wheat flour, or rye flour to achieve a rich color.
- ☐ When preparing yeast dough, use a glass measure and the temperature probe set at 120° to heat liquid and shortening.
- ☐ If you have a favorite yeast bread you wish to proof, follow directions in Caraway Rye Bread Ring (page 167).

Dandy Dumplings
Total Cooking Time: 17 to 19 minutes

  1 cup flour
1½ teaspoons baking powder
 ½ teaspoon salt
  3 tablespoons shortening
  1 tablespoon minced fresh
     parsley
 ⅔ cup milk
2½ cups chicken, beef, or
     vegetable broth

Measure flour, baking powder, and salt in mixing bowl. Cut in shortening until texture of cornmeal. Add parsley. Stir in milk to moisten, but batter should not be smooth. Pour stock in 1½-quart casserole. Cook on HI (max. power) 6 to 8 minutes, or until boiling. Drop dough by rounded teaspoon into boiling stock. Cook, uncovered, on HI (max. power) 6 minutes. Cook, covered, on HI (max. power) 5 minutes, or until dumplings are firm. Remove dumplings to serving dish with slotted spoon.

16 dumplings

COOKING/WARMING/DEFROSTING GUIDE —
CONVENIENCE BREADS

Food	Amount	Cook Control Setting	Time	Special Notes
Hamburger buns, hot dog rolls, frozen	1 lb.	30 (defrost)	3½ - 4½ minutes	Use original microproof container, paper plate, or towels. Place on microproof rack, turn over after 2 minutes.
Room temperature:	1	80 (reheat)	5 - 10 seconds	
	2	80 (reheat)	10 - 15 seconds	
	4	80 (reheat)	15 - 20 seconds	
	6	80 (reheat)	20 - 25 seconds	
Doughnuts, sweet rolls, muffins	1	80 (reheat)	10 - 15 seconds	Place on paper plate or towel. Add 15 seconds if frozen.
	2	80 (reheat)	20 - 25 seconds	
	4	80 (reheat)	35 - 40 seconds	
	6	80 (reheat)	45 - 50 seconds	
Whole coffee cake, frozen	10 - 13 oz.	80 (reheat)	1½ - 2 minutes	Place on paper plate or towel.
Room temperature:	10 - 13 oz.	80 (reheat)	1 - 1½ minutes	Place on paper plate or towel.
French bread, frozen	1 lb.	80 (reheat)	1½ - 2 minutes	Place on paper plate or towel.
Room temperature:	1 lb.	80 (reheat)	20 - 30 seconds	
English muffins, waffles, frozen	2	HI (max. power)	30 - 45 seconds	Place on paper towels. Toast in toaster after defrosting, if desired.
Corn bread mix	15 oz.	50 (simmer) HI (max. power)	10 minutes 3 - 4 minutes	Use 9″ round dish, paper-lined custard cups, or microproof muffin tray. Turn dish if rising unevenly. Let stand 5 minutes before serving.
Nut bread mix	6 muffins 15 - 17 oz.	HI (max. power) HI (max. power)	2 - 3 minutes 15 minutes	Let stand 2 minutes before serving. Use 1½-quart bowl with glass in center. Let stand 5 minutes before serving.
Blueberry muffin mix	4 6	HI (max. power) HI (max. power)	1¼ - 1½ minutes 2 - 3 minutes	Use paper-lined custard cups or microproof muffin tray. Let stand 2 minutes before serving.
Bread, frozen	1 slice	30 (defrost)	15 - 20 seconds	Place on paper plate or towels. Let stand 5 minutes before serving.
	1 lb. loaf	30 (defrost)	2 - 3 minutes	In original plastic bag, remove twister. Let stand 5 minutes before serving.
Coffeecake mix	19 oz.	50 (simmer) HI (max. power)	10 minutes 5 - 6 minutes.	Use 9″ round dish. Turn dish if rising unevenly. Let stand 5 minutes before serving.

Raisin-Nut Ring

Total Cooking Time: 9 to 12 minutes

Melt butter in 8-inch round glass dish on HI (max. power) 1 minute. Stir in sugar and corn syrup. Spread in dish. Sprinkle nuts and raisins evenly. Cook on HI (max. power) 1 minute. Place small beverage glass in center of dish and place biscuits around glass on brown sugar mixture. Bake on 50 (simmer) 7 to 10 minutes, or until biscuits are no longer doughy. If ring seems to be rising unevenly rotate dish. Remove glass. Invert ring onto serving plate, allow syrup to run over ring. Let stand 2 to 3 minutes before serving.

10 servings

3 tablespoons butter or margarine
⅓ cup brown sugar
2 tablespoons corn syrup
½ cup chopped nuts
¼ cup raisins
1 roll (10 ounces) refrigerated buttermilk biscuits

Onion Topped Bread

Total Cooking Time: 28 minutes

1 tablespoon unsalted
   shortening
1 loaf (1 pound) frozen
   bread dough
1 cup water
1 tablespoon melted butter or
   margarine
1 can fried onion rings,
   crushed

Grease generously with shortening an 8 × 4 × 2-inch microproof loaf pan. Place dough in pan. Pour water in 2-cup measure, cook on HI (max. power) 3 minutes, or until water boils. Place bread dough in oven with hot water. Set on Cook Control "1" (lowest power) for 20 minutes. Turn dough over after 10 minutes. Let stand in oven for 30 minutes longer, or until dough has risen about 1 inch above pan. Carefully brush melted butter on top of loaf and sprinkle with crushed onion rings. Remove water from oven. Return bread to oven. Cook on HI (max. power) 5 minutes. Let stand 10 minutes. Remove from pan and cool before slicing.

1 loaf

You can replace onion rings with a variety of toppings, such as taco seasoning, crushed cereal, cornmeal, cinnamon and sugar, or toasted sesame seeds.

The 30-minute standing time in the oven may be programmed by touching Clear, Time, 3, 0, 0, 0 and Cook Control 0.

Sour Cream Coffee Cake

Total Cooking Time: 8 minutes

½ cup butter or margarine,
   softened
½ cup sugar
2 eggs
½ teaspoon vanilla
1½ cups all-purpose flour
½ teaspoon baking soda
½ teaspoon baking powder
½ cup dairy sour cream

Topping:

⅓ cup brown sugar, packed
2 tablespoons all-purpose
   flour
½ cup chopped nuts
¼ teaspoon cinnamon
⅛ teaspoon salt
2 tablespoons butter or
   margarine

In medium bowl, cream butter and sugar. Add eggs and vanilla; mix well. Sift together flour, soda, and baking powder. Add to creamed mixture with sour cream. Set aside. Mix topping ingredients until crumbly. Spread half the batter in 8-inch microproof cake dish. Sprinkle half the topping mix over batter. Carefully spread remaining batter and sprinkle with all remaining topping. Cook on 60 (bake) 4 minutes. If cake is rising unevenly, rotate dish one-quarter turn. Cook on HI (max. power) 4 minutes, or until toothpick inserted in center comes out clean. Let stand 3 minutes before serving. Serve coffee cake warm.

9 servings

Banana Date Bread

Total Cooking Time: 16½ minutes

In large glass mixing bowl, melt butter on HI (max. power) 1½ minutes. With electric mixer, gradually beat in all remaining ingredients except dates. When smooth, stir in dates. Grease a 2-quart glass casserole and place a straight sided glass in center (or use a microproof ring mold). Pour batter around glass. Cook on 70 (roast) 15 minutes, or until toothpick inserted near center comes out clean. Rotate dish if bread seems to be rising unevenly. Let stand 10 minutes before twisting glass to remove and inverting dish on cooling rack. Cool before slicing.

8 to 10 servings

½ cup butter or margarine
½ cup brown sugar
2 eggs
2 cups sliced ripe bananas
   (2 medium)
2 cups all-purpose flour
½ teaspoon baking soda
1 teaspoon baking powder
½ teaspoon salt
1 teaspoon cinnamon
½ cup chopped dates

Caramel Nut Sticky Buns

Total Cooking Time: 3½ to 4 minutes

In 8-inch round glass dish combine butter, sugar, water, and cinnamon. Cook on HI (max. power) 1 minute. Stir as soon as butter is melted, then stir in nuts. Separate biscuits into ten, cutting each into quarters. Place in sugar mixture and stir carefully to coat each piece. Push biscuits toward outside of dish and place custard cup in center. Cook on HI (max. power) 2½ to 3 minutes. Remove custard cup and let buns stand 2 minutes before pulling sections apart and serving warm.

6 servings

3 tablespoons butter or
   margarine
⅓ cup brown sugar
1 tablespoon water
1 teaspoon cinnamon
⅓ cup chopped nuts
1 can (10 ounces)
   refrigerator biscuits

Garlic Parmesan Bread

Total Cooking Time: 1 to 2 minutes

Mix butter and garlic. Cut loaf into slices, 1-inch thick, without cutting all the way through the bottom crust. Spread slices of bread with garlic butter, then sprinkle with cheese and paprika. Place loaf on microproof rack or on paper towels. Cook on HI (max. power) 1 to 2 minutes, or until bread is heated through.

12 servings

½ cup (¼ pound) butter or
   margarine, softened
2 or 3 cloves garlic, minced
1 loaf (16 ounces) French,
   Italian, or sourdough
   bread
½ cup grated Parmesan cheese
   Paprika

Zucchini-Nut Bread

Total Cooking Time: 15 minutes

1 cup sugar, divided
2 teaspoons cinnamon
2 eggs
½ cup vegetable oil
½ cup yogurt
1 teaspoon vanilla
1 cup grated zucchini
1¾ cups all-purpose flour
1 teaspoon baking soda
1 teaspoon salt
⅔ cup chopped walnuts

Grease 6-cup microproof ring mold. Sprinkle mixture of 2 teaspoons of sugar and cinnamon over greased surface. Shake to spread evenly, discarding excess. Beat together eggs, remaining sugar, oil, yogurt, vanilla, and zucchini. Stir in remaining ingredients and mix well. Pour into prepared mold. Cook on 70 (roast) 15 minutes, or until toothpick inserted near center comes out clean. Rotate dish if bread appears to be rising unevenly. Let stand 10 minutes before removing from pan. Cool completely before slicing.

12 - 18 servings

Raisin Bran Muffins

Total Cooking Time: 6 to 9 minutes

1 egg
1 cup buttermilk
1¼ cups all-purpose flour
¾ cup brown sugar, packed
1 teaspoon baking soda
¼ teaspoon salt
1 cup raisin bran cereal
¼ cup vegetable oil
¼ cup chopped nuts (optional)

In small mixing bowl, beat egg and buttermilk. Mix in all other ingredients and stir well. Spoon batter into 6 paper-lined custard cups or microproof muffin pan; fill about half full. Cook 6 muffins at a time on HI (max. power) 2 to 3 minutes, or until no longer doughy. Repeat twice.

18 muffins

Oatmeal Muffins

Total Cooking Time: 6 to 9 minutes

2 eggs
⅔ cup brown sugar, packed
½ cup vegetable oil
½ cup buttermilk or sour milk
1 cup all-purpose flour
⅔ cup quick cooking oats
1 teaspoon baking powder
½ teaspoon baking soda
½ teaspoon salt

Topping

4 to 5 teaspoons brown sugar
3 tablespoons chopped nuts
   Nutmeg

In small mixing bowl beat eggs. Beat in brown sugar, oil, and buttermilk. Stir in, until just moistened, remaining ingredients except for topping ingredients. Spoon batter into 6 paper-lined custard cups or microproof muffin pan; fill about half full. Top each muffin with about ¼ teaspoon brown sugar, ½ teaspoon nuts, and a sprinkle of nutmeg. Cook on HI (max. power) 2 to 3 minutes, or until muffins are no longer doughy. Repeat twice. (Batter may be stored in refrigerator up to one week. Let come to room temperature, then cook as directed.)

18 muffins

Zucchini-Nut Bread, Raisin Bran Muffins, Oatmeal Muffins →

Brown and Serve Rolls

Total Cooking Time: 31 to 31½ minutes

3¼ to 3½ cups all-purpose
    flour, divided
1 teaspoon salt
1 tablespoon sugar
1 package (¼ ounce)
    active dry yeast
1 cup milk
3 tablespoons butter or
    margarine
1 egg, slightly beaten
1 tablespoon melted butter
    Celery, sesame, or poppy
    seeds

In large mixing bowl, combine 1½ cups of flour with salt, sugar, and yeast; mix well. In 2-cup measure, heat milk and butter, using the temperature probe on 70 (roast) set at 120°. Add warm milk mixture to dry ingredients. Beat in egg until smooth. Gradually add remaining flour to form a stiff dough. Knead until smooth and satiny, about 5 minutes. Place dough in greased glass bowl, turn dough to grease top. Cover with waxed paper. Place 1 cup water in 2-cup measure and bring to a boil on HI (max. power) 3 minutes. Place dough in oven next to water. (The hot water provides a moist, humid environment for the yeast to grow.) Set Cook Control at "1" for 10 minutes (this is the lowest energy setting available). Leave dough in oven for 20 minutes longer, or until double in volume. Turn dough onto floured surface and divide into 15 pieces. Grease a 10×6-inch glass baking dish. Form each of the 15 pieces into rolls and place in greased dish. Brush with melted butter and sprinkle with seeds. Again bring water to a boil on HI (max. power) 3 minutes. Place rolls in oven. Set Cook Control at "1" for 10 minutes. Leave rolls in oven for 20 minutes longer, or until double in volume. Remove water. Cook rolls on HI (max. power) 4½ to 5 minutes, or until no longer doughy. Remove rolls from pan and cool. The rolls may be browned later in the day, stored in the refrigerator for 2 to 3 days, or frozen for up to 3 months. To bake, preheat conventional oven to 425°. Room temperature rolls will take 7 minutes, refrigerated rolls 8 to 9 minutes, and frozen rolls 9 to 12 minutes. When done, they should be brown, and sound hollow when lightly tapped.

Caraway Rye Bread Ring

Total Cooking Time: 33½ to 34½ minutes

In large mixing bowl, combine 1½ cups of all-purpose flour with rye flour, yeast, sugar, salt, and caraway seeds. In 2-cup measure, heat water and 2 tablespoons butter, using temperature probe set at 120°. Pour into flour mixture, add molasses, and beat until smooth. Gradually add remaining flour to form a stiff dough. Knead until smooth and satiny, about 5 minutes. Place dough in greased glass bowl, turn dough to grease top. Place 1 cup water in 2-cup measure and bring to a boil on HI (max. power) 3 minutes. Place dough next to boiling water in oven. Set Cook Control at "1" (lowest power) for 10 minutes. Leave dough in oven for 20 minutes longer, or until double in volume. Turn dough onto floured surface and pat into rectangle 4×8 inches. Roll tightly to the long side and join ends to form circle. Grease 10-cup microproof bundt-type mold and sprinkle with cornmeal, shaking to spread evenly. In 1-cup glass measure melt 1 tablespoon butter on HI (max. power) 30 seconds. Place dough ring in pan, gently brush top with melted butter. Again heat 1 cup water on HI (max. power) 3 minutes and leave in oven. Place bread in oven. Set Cook Control at "1" (lowest power) for 10 minutes. Leave bread in oven for 20 minutes longer, or until double in volume. Remove water and cook on HI (max. power) 6 to 7 minutes, or until bread springs back when touched, sides recede from pan, and top is no longer doughy. Turn out on cooling rack. Cool before slicing.

8 to 10 servings

2½ to 3 cups all-purpose flour, divided
¾ cup rye flour
1 package (¼ ounce) active dry yeast
2 tablespoons brown sugar
½ teaspoon salt
2 teaspoons caraway seeds
1 cup water
3 tablespoons butter, divided
3 tablespoons dark molasses
2 tablespoons cornmeal

Country Cornbread

Total Cooking Time: 12 to 14 minutes

Mix dry ingredients in large mixing bowl. In small bowl combine remaining ingredients, then add to dry ingredients and stir until smooth. Pour into 8-inch glass baking dish. Cook on 50 (simmer) 10 minutes. Cook on HI (max. power) 2 to 4 minutes, or until a toothpick inserted in the middle comes out clean. Let stand 5 minutes before serving.

8 servings

1 cup all-purpose flour
1 cup cornmeal
3 tablespoons sugar
½ teaspoon salt
1 teaspoon baking powder
½ teaspoon baking soda
1 cup buttermilk or yogurt
2 tablespoons vegetable oil
2 eggs, slightly beaten

Desserts can transform a simple meal into a delectable feast. From baked fresh fruit to fudgy chocolate cake, they make the perfect ending to any meal. Here are some traditional family favorites, glamorous party desserts, and spur-of-the-moment treats. All are quick and easy with your microwave oven. In no time at all, cakes will rise before your eyes, custards will become thick and creamy, and pie fillings will bubble and thicken. Brownies and bar cookies are delicious, fast and fun to make, and if you've never tried homemade candies, now is the time! It's impossible to fail when you make candy the microwave way.

Yellow food coloring added to Homemade Pie Shell (page 175) will enhance the appearance. Chocolate wafer or graham cracker Crumb Crust (page 174) is a quick dessert when filled with pudding (top left). Rich Chocolate Fudge (page 179) is easy. A candy thermometer is used in the first step (top right) then other ingredients are added (above left). Microwave cakes rise higher than conventional. Fill cake pans only half-full (above right).

← *Devil's Food Cake (page 172) with Snow White Frosting (page 174), Coconut Squares (page 182), Date Oatmeal Bars (page 172)*

Converting Your Recipes

How easy it is! Puddings and custards can be baked without the usual water bath, and they need only occasional stirring. Fruits retain their bright color and fresh-picked flavor. Cakes cook so quickly; yet they are superior in texture, taste, and height. When you discover how effortless it is to make candy, you'll be trying all those recipes you've been longing to do. Because cakes and pie crusts cook so fast, they do not brown. If you like a browned surface, there are many ways to give desserts a browned look. So try adapting your dessert recipes following the guidance of a similar recipe here and these tips:

☐ You can enhance your light batter cookies and cakes with cinnamon, nutmeg, brown sugar, coffee, nuts, toppings, frostings, glazes, food coloring, etc.

☐ Small drop cookies and slice 'n bake cookies don't do as well as the larger bar cookies. Drop cookies must be cooked in small batches; they tend to cook unevenly, and need to be removed individually from the oven when finished.

☐ A serviceable cookie sheet can be made by covering cardboard with waxed paper.

☐ Layer cakes are generally baked one layer at a time. Baking is usually begun on 50 or 60 for the first 7 minutes, then finished on HI. If cake appears to be rising unevenly, rotate the dish one-quarter turn as necessary. Denser batters, such as fruit cakes and carrot cakes, require slower, gentler cooking. Set at 30 for good results.

☐ A pie shell is cooked when very slight browning occurs on top, and surface appears opaque and dry.

☐ For even cooking, select fruit of uniform size to be cooked whole, as in baked apples, or to be cooked in pieces, as in apple pie.

☐ Remove baked custards from oven when centers are nearly firm. They will continue to cook and set after removal.

☐ To avoid lumping, puddings should be stirred once or twice during the second half of cooking.

COOKING GUIDE — PUDDING AND PIE FILLING MIX

Food	Amount	Time (in minutes)	Cook Control Setting	Special Notes
Pudding and pie filling mix	3¼ ounces 5½ ounces	6½ - 7 8 - 10	HI (max. power) HI (max. power)	Follow package directions. Stir every 3 minutes. Use 4-cup glass measure.
Egg custard	3 ounces	8 - 10	70 (roast)	Follow package directions. Stir every 3 minutes. Use 4-cup glass measure.
Tapioca	3¼ ounces	6 - 7	HI (max. power)	Follow package directions. Stir every 3 minutes. Use 4-cup glass measure.

COOKING/DEFROSTING GUIDE — CONVENIENCE DESSERTS

Food	Amount	Cook Control Setting	Time	Special Notes
Brownies, other bars, frozen	12 - 13 oz.	30 (defrost)	2 - 3 minutes	In original ¾" foil tray, lid removed. Let stand 5 minutes.
Cookies, frozen	6	30 (defrost)	50 - 60 seconds	Place on paper plate or towels.
Pineapple upside-down cake mix	21½ oz.	50 (simmer) HI (max. power)	3 minutes 4 minutes	Use 9" round glass dish. Remove enough batter for 2 cupcakes, bake separately. Rotate if rising unevenly.
Cupcakes or crumb cakes, frozen	1 or 2	30 (defrost)	½ - 1 minute	Place on shallow plate.
Cheesecake, frozen	17 - 19 oz.	30 (defrost)	4 - 5 minutes	Remove from foil pan to plate. Let stand 1 minute.
Pound cake, frozen	10¾ oz.	30 (defrost)	2 minutes	Remove from foil pan to plate. Rotate once. Let stand 5 minutes.
Cake, frozen 2- or 3-layer	17 oz.	30 (defrost)	2½ - 3 minutes	Remove from foil pan to plate. Watch carefully, frosting melts fast. Let stand 5 minutes.
Custard pie, frozen	9" pie	70 (roast)	4 - 5½ minutes	Remove from foil pan to plate. Center should be nearly set.
Fruit pie, frozen, unbaked, 2 crusts	9" pie	HI (max. power)	13 - 15 minutes	On glass pie plate. Brown, if desired, in preheated 425° conventional oven 8 - 10 minutes.
Frozen fruit	10 oz.	HI (max. power)	5 - 5½ minutes	On microproof plate. Slit pouch. Flex halfway through cooking time to mix.
	16 oz.	HI (max. power)	7 - 9 minutes	Remove from bag. Place in glass casserole, cover. Stir halfway through cooking time.

Golden Apple Chunks

Total Cooking Time: 7 to 8 minutes

Place apples in 1-quart microproof casserole. Combine brown sugar and cinnamon in small bowl. Crumble over apples. Dot with butter. Cook, covered, on HI (max. power) 7 to 8 minutes, stirring after 4 minutes.

4 servings

4 medium cooking apples, peeled, quartered, and cored
¼ cup brown sugar, packed
1 teaspoon cinnamon
2 tablespoons butter or margarine

Fresh Strawberry Jam

Total Cooking Time: 20 to 23 minutes

In 4-quart microproof bowl combine fruit and juice with pectin. Cook, covered, on HI (max. power) 10 to 11 minutes, or until mixture boils. Stir once during cooking. Stir in sugar. Cook, uncovered, on HI (max. power) 10 to 12 minutes, or until mixture boils hard for at least 1 minute. Skim off any foam with metal spoon. Pour into hot sterilized glasses or jars and seal.

2 quarts

5 cups crushed strawberries, washed and hulled
2 teaspoons lemon juice
1 package (1¾ ounces) powdered fruit pectin
7 cups sugar

Devil's Food Cake

Total Cooking Time: 23 to 25 minutes

2 cups sifted all-purpose
   flour
1¼ teaspoons baking soda
 ¼ teaspoon salt
 ½ cup shortening
 2 cups sugar
 ½ cup cocoa
 1 teaspoon vanilla
 1 cup water
 ½ cup buttermilk
 2 eggs, beaten

Grease bottoms of two 8-inch round microproof cake pans. Line bottoms with waxed paper cut to size. Set aside. In large bowl, sift together flour, baking soda, and salt. Set aside. In separate large bowl, cream shortening, sugar, cocoa, and vanilla until light and fluffy. Pour water into 2-cup glass measure and cook on HI (max. power) 2½ minutes, or until water boils. Stir water, buttermilk, and eggs into creamed mixture. Beat well. Add all dry ingredients and beat until smooth. Pour batter equally into prepared cake pans. Cook, one pan at a time, on 50 (simmer) 8 minutes. Rotate pan one-quarter turn. Cook on HI (max. power) 1 to 2 minutes, or until toothpick inserted in center comes out clean. Remove from oven. Let stand 5 minutes. Invert onto cooling rack. Remove waxed paper. Let cool thoroughly before frosting.

8 to 10 servings

For frosting, try Chocolate Fudge Frosting (page 174) or use Snow White Frosting (page 174).

Date Oatmeal Bars

Total Cooking Time: 11 to 13 minutes

Filling

1 cup chopped dates
½ cup raisins
½ cup water
1 tablespoon all-purpose
   flour
2 tablespoons sugar
½ cup chopped nuts

Crust

½ cup butter or margarine
¼ teaspoon baking soda
1 tablespoon water
1 cup brown sugar
1 cup unsifted all-purpose
   flour
¼ teaspoon salt
1 cup quick-cooking rolled
   oats
1 teaspoon cinnamon

In glass bowl combine all filling ingredients except nuts. Cook, uncovered, on HI (max. power) 3 to 4 minutes, or until mixture boils and thickens, stirring once. The date filling should be the consistency of jam. Stir in nuts and set filling aside. In glass mixing bowl melt butter on HI (max. power) 1 minute. Dissolve soda in water and add to butter with all remaining ingredients except cinnamon. Firmly pat two-thirds of mixture in greased 9-inch round glass baking dish. Spread with date filling. Stir cinnamon into remaining oats mixture and crumble over top of filling. Cook, uncovered, on HI (max. power) 7 to 8 minutes, or until top no longer appears doughy. Rotate dish if mixture seems to be cooking unevenly. Cool on bread board, covered with foil, before cutting into squares.

24 bars

Poppy Seed Cake

Total Cooking Time: 7½ minutes

In 9-inch round glass baking dish, melt butter on HI (max. power) 30 seconds. Insert small straight-sided glass open side up in center. Sprinkle bottom of cake dish with mixture of cinnamon and sugar. Set aside. In electric mixer, beat cake mix and other ingredients on high 2 to 3 minutes (according to package directions). Pour batter in pan. Cook on 50 (simmer) 5 minutes, then on HI (max. power) 2 minutes, or until toothpick inserted in cake near center comes out slightly moist. If cake seems to be rising unevenly, rotate dish one-quarter turn during baking.

8 to 10 servings

2	teaspoons butter or margarine
2	teaspoons cinnamon
1½	teaspoons sugar
1	package (9 ounces) yellow cake mix
2	eggs
½	cup water, minus 1 tablespoon
5	tablespoons poppy seeds
¼	cup vegetable oil
5	tablespoons instant lemon pudding.

Chocolate Pudding Cake

Total Cooking Time: 9¾ to 11¾ minutes

Place butter in 1-cup glass measure. Cook on HI (max. power) 45 seconds, or until melted. In mixing bowl, sift flour, sugar, cocoa, baking powder, and salt. Stir in milk, melted butter, vanilla, and nuts. Pour into 8-inch round microproof baking dish. In 4-cup glass measure, mix brown sugar, cocoa, and water. Pour over batter. Do not stir. Cover with paper towel. Cook on HI (max. power) 9 to 11 minutes. Remove from oven and let stand 10 minutes. Top with whipped cream and serve.

9 servings

2	tablespoons butter
1	cup all-purpose flour
¾	cup sugar
2	tablespoons cocoa
2	teaspoons baking powder
½	teaspoon salt
½	cup milk
1	teaspoon vanilla
½	cup chopped nuts
¾	cup light brown sugar
¼	cup cocoa
1¼	cups water
	Whipped cream

Scotch Nut Oatmeal Cake

Total Cooking Time: 9¼ to 10¼ minutes

In 8-inch round glass baking dish, melt 2 tablespoons butter on HI (max. power) 45 seconds. Mix together brown sugar, butterscotch chips, and nuts. Spread evenly in bottom of dish, place small glass in center, open end up. Set aside. Heat water in glass mixing bowl on HI (max. power) 2 minutes, or until water boils. Stir in oats. Add butter pieces and let stand until butter is softened. Beat in sugars and egg. Stir in remaining ingredients just until blended. Pour over nut mixture in baking dish. Cook on HI (max. power) 6½ to 7½ minutes, or until cake springs back when lightly touched near center. Rotate dish during cooking if cake seems to be rising unevenly. Let stand 5 minutes to cool. Invert on serving plate and serve warm or chilled.

8 servings

2	tablespoons butter or margarine
¼	cup brown sugar, packed
¼	cup butterscotch chips
¼	cup chopped walnuts
¾	cup water
½	cup quick-cooking oatmeal
¼	cup butter or margarine, cut up
½	cup sugar
½	cup brown sugar, packed
1	egg
¾	cup all-purpose flour
½	teaspoon baking soda
½	teaspoon salt
½	teaspoon cinnamon
½	teaspoon nutmeg

Snow White Frosting

Total Cooking Time: 4 to 5 minutes

1 cup sugar
½ cup water
¼ teaspoon cream of tartar
   Dash salt
2 egg whites
1 teaspoon vanilla

In 2-cup glass measure combine sugar, water, cream of tartar, and salt. Insert temperature probe and cook on 70 (roast) set at 200°. In small mixing bowl, beat egg whites with electric mixer until soft peaks form. Gradually add hot syrup to egg whites, beating continuously. Continue beating 5 minutes, or until frosting is thick and fluffy. While beating, add vanilla.

1½ to 2 cups

Pecan Pie

Total Cooking Time: 9 to 10 minutes

¼ cup butter or margarine
1 cup sugar
½ cup dark corn syrup
3 eggs, slightly beaten
1 teaspoon vanilla
⅛ teaspoon salt
1¼ cups pecan halves
1 baked 9-inch Homemade
   Pie Shell (page 175)

In glass mixing bowl melt butter on HI (max. power) 1 minute. Add remaining ingredients, mix well. Pour into pastry shell. Cook on HI (max. power) 8 to 9 minutes, or until center is set. Let cool to room temperature or chill before serving.

8 servings

Chocolate Fudge Frosting

Total Cooking Time: 3½ to 4 minutes

1 square (1 ounce) baking
   chocolate
1 cup sugar
⅓ cup milk
¼ cup butter or margarine
⅛ teaspoon salt
1 teaspoon vanilla
¼ cup chopped nuts

In 4-cup glass measure or microproof mixing bowl, place chocolate, sugar, milk, butter, and salt. Cook on HI (max. power) for 2 to 2½ minutes, or until chocolate is melted. Stir to mix. Cook on HI (max. power) 1½ minutes, stirring after 1 minute. Add vanilla and beat with electric mixer until frosting is almost cool. Add nuts and beat until spreading consistency.

1 cup

Crumb Crust

Total Cooking Time: 2½ to 3 minutes

5 tablespoons butter or
   margarine
1¼ cups fine crumbs (vanilla
   wafers, graham crackers,
   gingersnaps, chocolate
   wafers, etc.)
1 tablespoon sugar

In 9-inch glass pie plate, melt butter on HI (max. power) 1 minute. Blend in crumbs and sugar. If desired, set aside 2 tablespoons crumb mixture to sprinkle over top of pie. Press crumb mixture firmly and evenly over bottom and sides of pie plate. Cook on HI (max. power) 1½ to 2 minutes. Cool before filling.

1 9-inch pie shell

Yogurt Pumpkin Pie

Total Cooking Time: 5 to 6 minutes

In 3-quart microproof bowl, mix pumpkin, brown sugar, cinnamon, nutmeg, ginger, and salt. Cook on HI (max. power) 1½ to 2 minutes, or until mixture begins to boil. Cool 10 minutes. Remove cover from frozen whipped topping and cook on 30 (defrost) 1 minute, or until it begins to thaw. Stir carefully. Fold thawed topping and yogurt into cooled pumpkin mixture. Spoon into pie shell. Refrigerate about 4 hours, or until set.

6 servings

1 cup canned or cooked
   pumpkin
¼ cup brown sugar, firmly
   packed
1 teaspoon cinnamon
½ teaspoon nutmeg
¼ teaspoon powdered ginger
¼ teaspoon salt
1 carton (9 ounces) frozen
   whipped topping
1 carton (8 ounces) vanilla
   yogurt
1 9-inch Crumb Crust
   (page 174)

Homemade Pie Shell

Total Cooking Time: 6 to 7 minutes

Place flour and salt in small bowl. With pastry blender or two knives cut in shortening until mixture resembles small peas. Sprinkle water over mixture. Stir with fork to form a ball. Roll out on floured pastry board with rolling pin to about 12-inch circle. Fit into glass 9-inch pie plate. Trim and flute edge. Prick pastry with fork. Cook on HI (max. power) 6 to 7 minutes. Pastry is done when it looks dry and blistered and is not doughy. Cool. Add filling.

1 9-inch pie shell

1 cup all-purpose flour
1 teaspoon salt
6 tablespoons shortening
2 tablespoons ice water

Danish Apple Pie

Total Cooking Time: 12 to 14 minutes

Place apple slices in large mixing bowl. Mix sugar, flour, salt, and cinnamon; add to apples and stir to coat. Pour apples into baked pastry shell, spread evenly. Mix together remaining ingredients for topping and sprinkle over apples. Cook on HI (max. power) 12 to 14 minutes, or until apples are fork-tender. Cool before serving.

6 to 8 servings

7 cooking apples, peeled
   cored, and sliced
   (6 cups)
¾ cup sugar
2 tablespoons flour
⅛ teaspoon salt
1 teaspoon cinnamon
1 baked 9-inch Homemade
   Pie Shell (above)
2 tablespoons butter or
   margarine
¼ cup all-purpose flour
¼ cup brown sugar

Baked Maple Bananas

Total Cooking Time: 3 minutes

2 tablespoons butter or
    margarine
3 tablespoons maple syrup
4 bananas, peeled, cut in
    half and sliced
    lengthwise
1 tablespoon lemon juice

In medium-size microproof baking dish, cook butter on HI (max. power) 30 seconds, or until melted. Stir in maple syrup. Place bananas in dish, coat well with butter mixture, using spoon. Cook on HI (max. power) 1 minute. Turn bananas, cook on HI (max. power) 1½ minutes. Sprinkle with lemon juice and serve warm.

4 servings

You may also cook whole bananas and cut them in serving portions at the table.

Lemon Pineapple Crème

Total Cooking Time: 5 to 6 minutes

¾ cup sugar, divided
3 tablespoons cornstarch
1 can (8 ounces) crushed
    pineapple, undrained
⅔ cup water
2 eggs, separated
1 teaspoon grated lemon peel
2 tablespoons lemon juice
1 package (3 ounces) cream
    cheese, cubed

In 4-cup glass measure, mix ½ cup of sugar, the cornstarch, pineapple and its juice, and water. Cook, uncovered, on HI (max. power) 4 to 5 minutes, or until mixture boils. Stir twice during cooking time. Beat egg yolks. Stir into pineapple mixture the lemon peel, juice, and egg yolks, then cream cheese. Cook, uncovered, on 80 (reheat) 1 minute. Beat with electric mixer to blend in cream cheese. Cool. Beat egg whites until frothy, gradually add ¼ cup of sugar until soft peaks form. Fold into cooled pudding. Spoon into dessert dishes and refrigerate until served.

5 to 6 servings

Baked Apple

Total Cooking Time: 4 to 5 minutes

2 large baking apples
2 teaspoons butter or
    margarine
4 teaspoons brown sugar
¼ teaspoon cinnamon
2 teaspoons golden raisins
2 tablespoons water

Core apples and make a slit in skin all around the middle of each apple to prevent skin from bursting. Place apples in small microproof baking dish. In small bowl melt butter on HI (max. power) 10 seconds. Stir in sugar, cinnamon, and raisins. Fill each apple with sugar mixture. Add water to dish. Cook, covered with plastic wrap, on HI (max. power) 4 to 5 minutes.

2 servings

Try this recipe with two firm pears instead of apples for a special treat.

Lemon Pineapple Crème, Baked Maple Bananas →

Applesauce

Total Cooking Time: 10 to 12 minutes

6 cups peeled, cored, and
   sliced cooking apples
½ cup water
1 tablespoon lemon juice
¼ cup sugar
½ teaspoon cinnamon or
   nutmeg

In 2-quart microproof casserole, mix apples, water, and lemon juice. Cook, covered, on HI (max. power) 10 to 12 minutes, or until apples are tender. Stir in remaining ingredients until smooth. Serve warm or cold with pork or as a light dessert.

4 to 6 servings

Cherry Crunch

Total Cooking Time: 12 to 14 minutes

1 package (9 ounces) white or
   yellow single-layer
   cake mix
¼ cup chopped nuts
2 tablespoons brown sugar,
   packed
2 teaspoons cinnamon
1 can (21 ounces) cherry
   pie filling
½ cup butter or margarine,
   melted

In a bowl, combine dry cake mix, nuts, brown sugar, and cinnamon. In an 8-inch glass baking dish, spoon cherry pie filling into bottom. Sprinkle cake mix mixture evenly over pie filling. Drizzle melted butter over top. Cook on HI (max. power) 12 to 14 minutes, or until topping is no longer doughy. Rotate dish during cooking if cake does not appear to be rising evenly. Let stand 5 minutes. Serve warm with whipped cream or vanilla ice cream.

6 to 8 servings

Cranapple Jelly

Total Cooking Time: 21 to 25 minutes

4 cups cranapple juice
1 package (1¾ ounces)
   powdered fruit pectin
4 cups sugar

Combine juice and pectin in 3-quart glass bowl. Cook, covered, on HI (max. power) 11 to 13 minutes, or until mixture boils. Stir once during cooking. Stir in sugar. Cook, uncovered, on HI (max. power) 10 to 12 minutes, or until mixture boils hard for at least 1 minute. Skim off any foam with metal spoon. Pour into hot sterilized glasses or jars and seal.

6 cups

Tapioca Pudding

Total Cooking Time: 6 minutes

1 package (3¼ ounces)
   tapioca pudding mix
2 cups milk

Mix tapioca and milk in 4-cup glass measure. Cook on HI (max. power) 4 minutes. Stir, cook on HI (max. power) 2 minutes, or until mixture comes to full boil. Pour into serving dishes and cool.

4 servings

Raisin Bread Pudding

Total Cooking Time: 16½ to 19 minutes

In ungreased 2-quart round microproof dish, mix bread and raisins. Beat eggs, sugar, vanilla, and salt until well blended. In 4-cup glass measure heat milk and butter on HI (max. power) 4½ to 5 minutes, or until steaming hot. Gradually stir in egg mixture. Pour over bread and raisins, sprinkle with cinnamon. Cover with waxed paper. Cook on 50 (simmer) 12 to 14 minutes. When cooked, center may be slightly soft but will set as pudding cools. Serve warm or chilled.

6 servings

4 slices raisin bread, cubed
   (about 4 cups)
¼ cup raisins
3 eggs
½ cup brown sugar, packed
1 teaspoon vanilla
  Dash salt
2 cups milk
2 tablespoons butter or
   margarine
  Cinnamon or nutmeg

Peanut Brittle

Total Cooking Time: 18 to 20 minutes

Place sugar, corn syrup, water, salt, and peanuts in 2-quart microproof bowl or casserole. Cook on HI (max. power) 5 minutes, then stir. Cook on HI (max. power) 13 to 15 minutes, or until syrup separates into threads. This is the hard-crack stage, or 300° on a candy thermometer. Check temperature with thermometer several times during the last few minutes. (Do not leave thermometer in oven while cooking.) Stir in butter, baking soda, and vanilla just until light and bubbly. Pour onto buttered cookie sheet. Spread. Cool and break into pieces.

1¼ pounds

1½ cups sugar
½ cup corn syrup
½ cup water
  Dash salt
2 cups raw peanuts
1 tablespoon butter or
   margarine
1 teaspoon baking soda
1 teaspoon vanilla

You can use dark or light corn syrup. Obviously, the color of your peanut brittle will differ, but both are delicious.

Rich Chocolate Fudge

Total Cooking Time: 20 to 22 minutes

In 4-quart microproof bowl, mix sugar, milk, and butter. Cook on HI (max. power) 20 to 22 minutes, or until a few drops of mixture in cold water forms a soft ball (234° on candy thermometer). Do not leave thermometer in oven while cooking. Stir well every 5 minutes during cooking. Stir in chocolate bits and marshmallow creme until mixture is well blended. Add vanilla and nuts, mix. Pour into buttered 9-inch square dish for thick pieces or 12 × 7 × 2-inch dish for thinner pieces. Cool and cut into squares.

48 pieces

4 cups sugar
1 can (14 ounces) evaporated
   milk
1 cup butter or margarine
1 package (12 ounces) semi-
   sweet chocolate bits
1 jar (7 ounces) marshmallow
   creme
1 teaspoon vanilla
1 cup chopped nuts

Rocky Road Candy

Total Cooking Time: 5 minutes

1 package (12 ounces) semi-
  sweet chocolate chips
1 package (12 ounces)
  butterscotch chips
½ cup butter
1 package (10½ ounces)
  miniature marshmallows
1 cup nuts

In 4-quart microproof mixing bowl combine chocolate, butterscotch, and butter. Cook on 70 (roast) 5 minutes, or until melted. Stir. Fold in marshmallows and nuts. Spread on buttered 13×9-inch pan. Refrigerate until set (about 2 hours). Cut into squares.

45 servings

Try these variations: Substitute ½ cup nuts and ½ cup chopped dried fruit or 1 cup chopped dried fruit for 1 cup nuts. Dried apricots, pitted prunes, or candied fruit would be delicious.

Almond Bark

Total Cooking Time: 6½ to 8½ minutes

1 cup whole blanched almonds
1 teaspoon butter or
  margarine
1 pound white chocolate

In 9-inch glass pie plate place almonds and butter. Cook on HI (max. power) 4 to 5½ minutes, or until almonds are toasted, stirring twice during cooking. Set aside. Place chocolate in large microproof mixing bowl and cook on HI (max. power) 2½ to 3 minutes, or until softened. Stir in almonds and pour onto waxed paper-lined baking sheet. Spread to desired thickness and refrigerate until set. Break into pieces to serve.

1½ pounds

Mints

Total Cooking Time: 5 to 6 minutes

2 cups sugar
¼ cup light corn syrup
¼ cup milk
¼ teaspoon cream of tartar
  Peppermint extract
  Red or green food coloring

In 2-quart glass measure, combine sugar, corn syrup, milk, and cream of tartar. Cook on HI (max. power) 5 to 6 minutes or until a few drops of mixture in cold water forms a soft ball (238° on candy thermometer). Let stand 3 minutes to cool slightly. Beat with electric mixer until creamy. Flavor with 8 to 10 drops peppermint extract and color with food coloring. Drop mixture by teaspoonfuls onto foil. When cool, store in airtight container.

36 servings

Rocky Road Candy, Almond Bark, Mints →

Coconut Squares

Total Cooking Time: 8 minutes

¼ cup butter or margarine
1 cup graham cracker crumbs
1 teaspoon sugar
1 cup flaked coconut
⅔ cup sweetened condensed
   milk
½ cup chopped nuts
1 cup semi-sweet chocolate
   bits

Place butter in 9-inch round microproof baking dish. Cook on HI (max. power) 1 minute, or until melted. Stir in crumbs and sugar. Pat mixture firmly and evenly in bottom of dish. Cook on HI (max. power) 2 minutes. Cool partially. Mix coconut, milk, and nuts. Spoon carefully over graham cracker crust. Cook on HI (max. power) 4 minutes, rotating dish one-half turn once during cooking. Sprinkle with chocolate bits. Cook on HI (max. power) 1 minute. Spread melted chocolate evenly over coconut mixture. Cool and cut into squares.

16 to 20 squares

Peanut Crispy Bars

Total Cooking Time: 3 to 3½ minutes

¼ cup butter or margarine
5 cups miniature or 40 large
   marshmallows
⅓ cup peanut butter
5 cups crispy rice cereal
1 cup peanuts, dry roasted,
   unsalted

In 3-quart microproof casserole, melt butter on HI (max. power) 1 minute. Add marshmallows and cook, covered, on HI (max. power) 2 to 2½ minutes, or until soft, stirring once. Stir in peanut butter until smooth. Mix in cereal and peanuts. Press warm mixture into lightly buttered 12 × 7 × 2-inch dish. Cool and cut into bars.

36 bars

Double Chocolate Brownies

Total Cooking Time: 7½ minutes

½ cup butter or margarine
2 ounces unsweetened baking
   chocolate
2 eggs
¾ cup sugar
½ cup all-purpose flour
1 teaspoon baking powder
1 teaspoon vanilla
1 cup chopped nuts
1 cup chocolate chips
   Powdered sugar

In 2-cup glass measure place butter and chocolate and cook on HI (max. power) 1½ minutes, or until butter is melted. Chocolate will not appear melted until stirred. Beat eggs in large mixing bowl until light and foamy. Stir in chocolate mixture, sugar, flour, baking powder, and vanilla. Stir in nuts and chocolate chips. Pour into 9-inch microproof baking dish. Cook on HI (max. power) 6 minutes. Brownies will still be moist but will firm as cooled. Sprinkle with powdered sugar. Cool before cutting into squares.

18 to 20 servings

Dinner's in the oven! Who doesn't look forward to hearing this familiar saying as mealtime approaches? You'll find that just as in conventional cooking you can prepare a whole two- or three-dish meal at the same time in your microwave oven. For the most successful whole meal, it is important to consider the placement of dishes in the oven, the size and shape of the microproof containers, the kinds of food you select, the timing, and the sequence of cooking. This chapter provides you with all the necessary information and step-by-step instructions for organizing your own whole meals. Start by reading the following basic tips on how to approach whole meal planning:

- ☐ Since microwaves enter from the top of the oven, they are primarily attracted to food placed on the middle metal rack; a smaller amount reaches the bottom tray. It is logical then to place delicate quick-cooking food on the bottom glass tray and longer cooking food on the middle metal rack.
- ☐ Whenever the metal middle rack is not being used, remove it from oven.
- ☐ When the browning dish or grill is used, place it on the bottom glass tray. Do not cook other foods on the bottom glass tray at the same time.
- ☐ An ideal procedure for whole-meal cooking is to place two foods with similar cooking times on the middle metal rack and one shorter cooking food on the bottom tray.
- ☐ If all foods require the same cooking time, reverse the location of dishes in the oven halfway through cooking period.
- ☐ While the middle rack can be used in two positions, the upper position is generally best. use the lower position whenever greater capacity on the top is needed. This does limit the usable space below.
- ☐ Check your cooking dishes to be sure they will fit together on a shelf before filling with food.
- ☐ Often covers with knobs are too high to fit easily when the middle metal rack is used. Use plastic wrap instead of casserole lids when necessary.

IMPORTANT GUIDELINES FOR TIMING AND PLANNING

- ☐ If all foods take less than 15 minutes individually, add cooking times together and program the menu for the total time.
- ☐ If all foods take 15 to 35 minutes individually, add cooking times together and subtract about 5 minutes.
- ☐ If any one food takes over 35 minutes, all the food can be cooked in the time suggested for food taking the longest time.

In order to make the timing and planning easier, we have divided the menus into two types: one-stage and two-stage. For one-stage menus, all the dishes are cooked for the same length of time. The two-stage menus require partial cooking of one main dish and then the addition of other dishes to the oven.

Tips to remember in planning a one- or two-stage menu:

1. Choose a menu from the chart.
2. Review the individual recipe. Occasionally you will find that an ingredient should be prepared ahead; for example, squash is precooked 2 minutes to be more easily cut for Baked Acorn Squash (page 146).
3. Check microproof dishes to be sure they fit in the oven together. Change dish sizes, if needed.
4. Place dishes in oven with food from column "A" on the middle metal rack; "B" and "C" are placed on the bottom glass tray.
5. Apply the rules in "Important Guidelines for Timing and Planning." Cooking time for each recipe follows the recipe title in the menu charts.
6. Most recipes in whole-meal cooking benefit from stirring, rearranging, or turning about halfway through cooking time.

ONE-STAGE MENUS
Pick one dish from each column in any combination.

A	B	C
All-American Meatballs (14) (page 78)	Corn-Mushroom Scallop (9) (page 147)	Crumb Topped Tomatoes (4) (page 145)
Favorite Meat Loaf (30) (page 79)	Parsley New Potatoes (12) (page 150)	Frozen Fruit 10 oz. (6) (page 171)
Simple Salmon Loaf (30) (page 115)	Broccoli Spears 10 oz. Frozen (10) (page 139)	Lemon Butter Sauce (2) (page 153)
Pot Roast in Sherry (50) (page 75)	Corn and Pepper Pudding (19) (page 146)	Cherry Crunch (14) (page 178)
Orange Ginger Pork Chops (22) (page 87)	Pan Baked Potato Halves (12) (page 150)	Carrots 10 oz. Frozen (9) (page 139)
Barbecued Chicken (20) (page 100)	Stuffing Mix 6 oz. pkg. (5) (page 141)	Broccoli 10 oz. Frozen (8) (page 139)

To demonstrate one-stage menu planning we have chosen:

(A) All-American Meatballs
    page 78 .... 14 min.
(B) Corn-Mushroom Scallop
    page 147 ...... 9 min.
(C) Crumb Topped Tomatoes
    page 145 ...... $4\frac{1}{2}$ min.

Note that each individual cooking time takes less than 15 minutes. Using the "Guidelines" (page 183), this one-stage meal will cook in $27\frac{1}{2}$ minutes.

Let's take it step by step:

1. Prepare the All-American Meatballs according to the recipe, omitting the cornstarch and water at this time. Cover with plastic wrap, set aside.
2. Prepare Corn-Mushroom Scallop in 8 × 4-inch loaf pan. Omit topping of $\frac{1}{4}$ cup of crumbs and butter at

this time. Cover with plastic wrap, set aside.

3. Prepare the Crumb Topped Tomatoes on 9-inch pie plate.
4. Place middle metal rack in oven, Place meatballs on rack.

Place corn dish and tomato dish on bottom glass tray. Cook on HI (max. power) 27 minutes. After 10 minutes of cooking stir cornstarch and water into meatballs and cover. Stir scalloped corn and cover.

5. Remove from oven and top corn with ¼ cup of crumbs dotted with butter. Let all dishes stand, covered, on heat-resistant surface for 5 minutes before serving.

TWO-STAGE MENUS

Pick one dish from each column in any combination.

A	B	C
Tomato Swiss Steak (55) (page 78)	Parsley New Potatoes (12) (page 150)	Poppy Seed Cake (7½) (page 173)
Lamb Ragout (45) (page 90)	Country Cornbread (14) (page 167)	Frozen Fruit 16 oz. (9) (page 171)
Baked Ham with Pineapple (29) (page 87)	Baked Acorn Squash (16) (page 146)	Golden Apple Chunks (8) (page 171)
Chicken and Vegetables (21) (page 101)	Baked Apple (5) (page 176)	Hard Roll, heat - last 3 min.

Standing time is especially important in whole meal cooking. The Swiss Steak whole meal (above) finishes cooking during standing time (left).

The Two-Stage procedure is designed to give one recipe a longer time to cook. To demonstrate this we have chosen:

(A) Tomato Swiss Steak
      page 78 .... 55 min.
(B) Parsley New Potatoes
      page 150 ...... 12 min.
(C) Poppy Seed Cake
      page 173 .... 7½ min.

Using the "Guidelines" (page 183), all foods will be cooked in the time it takes Tomato Swiss Steak, 55 minutes.

Let's take it step by step:

1. Melt butter for cake and set aside.
2. Prepare Tomato Swiss Steak. Place on bottom glass tray and cook, covered, on HI (max. power) 5 minutes.
3. Meanwhile, prepare Parsley New Potatoes. Place in 8×5-inch loaf pan, covered with plastic wrap, and set aside.
4. Prepare Poppy Seed Cake.
5. Place middle metal rack in oven. Place steak on middle rack, potatoes and cake on bottom glass tray.
6. Cook on HI (max. power) 30 minutes. Rearrange steak, cover. Stir potatoes, cover. If cake is rising unevenly, rotate dish.
7. Cook on HI (max. power) 20 to 25 minutes, or until steak is cooked. Remove from oven. Drain potatoes, stir in butter, parsley, salt, and pepper. Let all dishes stand 5 minutes before serving.

TEMPERATURE PROBE MENUS
Pick one dish from each column in any combination.

A	B	C

Pork Loin, boneless (165°)
   3 to 4 lb.   (page 71)
Beef Rib-eye roast (130°)
   boneless - 2½ to 3 lbs.   (page 69)
Tenderloin of Beef Supreme (130°)
   (page 74)
Turkey Roast - thawed (150°)
   2 to 3 lbs.   (page 94)
Whole Chicken (180°)
   3 lbs.   (page 94)
	Corn and Pepper Pudding
	   (page 146)
	Pan-Baked Potato Halves
	   (page 150)
	Twice-Baked Potatoes
	   2 to 2½ lbs. (page 148)
	Candied Sweet Potatoes
	   (pre-bake potato) (page 147)
	Creamed Potatoes
	   4.7 oz. pkg. (page 141)
		Applesauce
		   (page 178)
		Green Beans, fresh
		   (page 139)
		Peas Francine
		   (page 143)
		Stuffing Mix
		   6 oz. pkg. (page 141)
		Green Beans Italian
		   (page 148)

Another whole meal method is the use of the temperature probe. All the food will be finished when the meat is ready. HI (max. power) is used, even though the individual recipes may call for lower power settings. The Temperature Setting to use follows the meat recipe title.

Protect top of meat with a narrow strip of foil, and place on middle rack. Arrange accompanying dishes on bottom tray. Turn meat over halfway through cooking. Stir or rearrange vegetables or other dishes at the same time. Cover as required by the individual recipe.

Parsley New Potatoes (page 150), Poppy Seed Cake →
(page 173), Tomato Swiss Steak (page 78), Whole Meal
Directions (page 185)

With practice and imagination you will enjoy trying different combinations. For example, here is a special menu method that puts the meat on the bottom glass tray for the second stage to give it a simmer effect, while the microwave energy is concentrated on the vegetables.

Country Style Ribs
    page 82 .... 60 min.
4 Corn-on-the-Cob
    page 140 .... 12 min.
4 Baked Potatoes (6 oz. each)
    page 140 .... 12 min.

Let's take it step by step:

1. Prepare Country Style Ribs. Cook on 70 (roast) 25 minutes, drain.
2. Meanwhile, remove husks and silk from each ear of corn. Wrap each ear individually in waxed paper.
3. Wash and remove any blemishes from potatoes, pierce. Brush both sides of ribs with sauce, cover with plastic wrap.

4. Place middle metal rack in oven. Place ribs on bottom glass tray. Place corn, spoke fashion, on middle rack; place one potato between each ear of corn. Cook on HI (max. power) 30 to 35 minutes, or until cooked. Turn vegetables over after 15 minutes.
5. Let stand, covered, 5 minutes before serving.

INDEX